1985

*To Lee
a beloved teacher!
Ruth*

A WOMAN'S WALDEN

Dedication

To
my husband, Ólaf
and our sons,
Linae, Loren, Jon, David.

A WOMAN'S WALDEN

by Ruthe T. Spinnanger
author of *Better Than Divorce*

Bridge Publishing, Inc.
Publishers of:
LOGOS • HAVEN • OPEN SCROLL

A Woman's Walden
Copyright © 1984 by Bridge Publishing, Inc.
All rights reserved
Printed in the United States of America
Library of Congress Catalog Card Number: 84-71120
International Standard Book Number: 0-88270-554-7
Bridge Publishing, Inc., South Plainfield, New Jersey 07080

Contents

1. "Delicate Handling" 1
2. "Thumbnail Living" 7
3. At a Standstill 15
4. Home: Our First Paradise 19
5. "Where I Lived and What I Lived For" 25
6. Reading 37
7. Leisure 43
8. Socializing 49
9. Guests 53
10. Gardening 61
11. Neighbors 69
12. Retirement Village, U.S.A. 75
13. Former Inhabitants 85
14. The Pond 91
15. Jack's Pond 97
16. Dual Urges 101
17. The "Smoke-Self" 109
18. Symbolic Activities 117
19. Summer Locked Up 127
20. "The Green Blade" 133
    Poems 147
    Notes 171

Permissions

Grateful acknowledgment is made to the following publishers for permission to quote from their published materials and texts:

The New American Library, for *Walden*, by Henry David Thoreau, First Printing, 1942.

The Oxford University Press, for *The Poems of Gerard Manley Hopkins*, edited by W.H. Gardner and N.H. Mackenzie, 1967.

New Directions Press, for *New Seeds of Contemplation*, by Thomas Merton, 1972.

Random House Publishers, for *Future Shock*, by Alvin Toffler, 1970.

Random House Publishers, for *The Selected Writings of Emerson*, Edited by Brooks Atkinson, 1950.

Harcourt, Brace and World, for Louis Untermeyer, in *Modern British Poetry*, 1962.

Macmillan Co., for *The Golden Bough*, by Sir James George Frazer, 1971.

Scott, Foresman and Co., *Freedom of Dilemme: Readings in Mass Media*, edited by David J. Riley, 1971.

Lane Books, for *Basic Gardening*, 1971.

West Pasco Historical Society, for quotations from *West Pasco's Heritage*, 1974.

University of Texas Press, for quotations from *The Florida of the Inca*, by the Inca, Garcilosa de la Vega, translated and edited by John Grier and Jeannette Johnson Varner, 1951.

Dell Publishing, Co., for quotations from *Thoughts in Solitude*, by Thomas Merton, 1961.

Alfred Knopf, Inc., for quotations from *The Uses of Enchantment*, by Bruno Bettelheim, 1977.

W.W. Norton Publishers, *The Self Conceived*, by Helen Morgan, 1974.

Encyclopaedia Britannica, Inc., *A Syntopicon of Great Books of the Western World*, Mortimer J. Adler, William Gorman, editors, 1952.

Acknowledgments

Since very little writing is ever a monologue, it is impossible to acknowledge all whose influences are woven into these pages. Many writers and many people have had an impact on my thinking and to make specific references to such influences would be an impossible task. Yet only the faith of those who support a writer can turn such a one into an author. Browning claimed that a writer becomes a writer only on the back of another writer, and in his well-known work, *The Ring and The Book*, he converts a Roman murder story into a 690-page poem as proof of his claim. His example, as well as the encouragement of my husband, and my friend and typist, Bernice Johnson, are among the influences that made this book a reality. However, the book would never have seen print without the belief and guidance of my publisher, Lloyd B. Hildebrand. Nor would I omit to include my enduring thanks to the unsung readers of my unpublished manuscript: Dr. E. De Groot; Dr. and Mrs. William Kalosieh (my friends, Roselle and Bill); Jean Abrahamson, a colleague; Margaret Graham, author; and my beloved Superintendent, Carl Padovano, and Chairman of English, Mateo Picarelli, who, along with the Board of Education of Hackensack High School so graciously granted me two years' leave of absence in which to write this book.

Introduction

"As long as possible," writes Henry David Thoreau in 1854, "live free and uncommitted"; for him this meant a two-year stay at Walden Pond in a tiny hut. But is such a goal desirable or even possible today? We have homes to maintain, children to raise, careers to develop, payments to meet—responsibilities in abundance. What price, freedom?

This is the question Ruthe Spinnanger sets out to explore in a year's planned "retreat" from her home in New Jersey to a Florida cottage. Here she tries to live deliberately—to discover reality. Though she understates it, hers is a religious quest, as well as flight from what Thoreau calls the "St. Vitus dance" of daily living.

Walden is actually an examination of current value systems. On his sunlit shores, Thoreau cut expenses to gain the necessary leisure for reading and meditation. Though never intending to make Walden a lifelong hermitage, he found it a vantage point for comment on the futility of war, on the low level of culture and the trashiness of popular reading, on an experiment with vegetarianism as a way of holiness. Ultimately, he hoped for self-discovery—a revelation of the nature of the self and its relation to the world, the universe, and God.

Using *Walden* as her model, Ruthe Spinnanger turns a sabbatical year into a period of self-examination and a search for truth. In her activities she is joyfully human; she tends her

A WOMAN'S WALDEN

garden, bakes bread, takes early morning walks, sits meditatively in a grove of pines, notes the passing of seasons, but through the exercise of her imagination she is a shaper and molder of the experience, while at the same time her record shows how this experience is forming her. Like Thoreau, she develops a perspective which produces some surprising comments on American values.

"You will know the truth and the truth will set you free." How, then, can we know? Thoreau makes clear that re-evaluation leads to rebirth. In spring, when the pond thaws after a cold winter, he notes the re-vitalization of the earth and identifies with it: "Walden was dead and is alive again!" Ruthe Spinnanger experiments with simple, austere patterns of living and discovers that losing leads to finding.

Elizabeth M. De Groot
Professor of English
The William Paterson College
of New Jersey

Chapter 1
"Delicate Handling"

The finest qualities of our nature, like the bloom on fruits, can be preserved only by the most delicate handling. Yet we do not treat ourselves nor one another thus tenderly.[1]

Caught—. Caught in an age of change, changing changelessly. Torn by self-made over-commitments. Snared in a web of over-choice. Fragmented by multiplied activities. Being busy: hailed as God's medicine, with no questions asked as to whether such busyness ever can degenerate into socially-pressured over-activity.

Did my actions take their values, their sense of worthwhileness from opinion polls rather than from the unpopular and alien view of the heart? To suit our actions to our thoughts and our thoughts to our actions is too often viewed as merely willful nonconformity. Worse, it might lead to the curse of inactivity, to that "devil's workshop," idleness. The wisdom that declares that our "strength is to sit still,"[2] is regarded as outmoded, and—above all—impractical.

Surely we are faced with options no other age has had to face and confronted with too many diverging roads that alluringly beckon. Flying over our great land, one can note that it is bound round with what looks like black spaghetti, a creeping macadam that should cause us to question whether humanity can keep pace

A WOMAN'S WALDEN

with its own technology. We stifle those promises that are made and broken only because they are made to ourselves. We vow that we will have more time in a mythical "sometime," in a tomorrow that never comes. It is a tomorrow that may once have crept in a "petty pace" but now races again and again to a victorious today until we shake our heads asking, "What happened to our promised 'tomorrow' "?

Does the mind-reeling trapeze act that modern man performs in the multiplicity of his involvement anywhere include an oasis of simplicity? Could Thoreau's advice be followed in the twentieth century? His words, "As long as possible live free and uncommitted,"[3] nagged at my own sense of fragmentation. And what of that "delicate handling" he recommends?

In my head I often argue with him. How can I give myself the same careful-not-to-bruise handling that I give to grapes? Unlike a grape, I have several functions: wife, mother, teacher, nurse, cook, writer, musician, housekeeper, secretary, accountant, hostess, gardener, hiker, traveler, shopper, seamstress, and interior decorator. No cry of discrimination can change the fact that my role as a wife gives me the identity of wife, just as my maternal obligations grant me the identity of mother.

Yet in each of these roles I recognize an element outside of myself. Something external directs me. Too many required actions become no more than a mask for the inner self. To uncover those role-masks and to simplify my life, I must free myself of multiplied demands on my time.

Did this mean I had to abandon my husband, my family, my profession? By no means. I decided to reduce all my activities, including my financial accounts, until they fit, as Thoreau said, on my "thumbnail." It meant that I had to settle for a less-than-poverty-level income, that level having been set by the government.

Having done that, would it be necessary for me to take to the woods, grow my own food and spin my own wool? The spinning

"Delicate Handling"

wheel in the family room presented an inviting prospect. Just imagine owning a piece of cloth made from wool that you had spun, spooled, warped, loomed and woven. Instead of making me a "tool of my tools," such activity would make me merely a "tool" of misguided primitivism. Instead of simplifying my life, I would be multiplying its complexities. No. I refused to romanticize an earlier age. I would simplify in the context of this present day.

How should I answer Thoreau's claim that "we are tools of our tools"?[4] I decided to strip myself of as many conveniences as possible and examine my own dependence on them from the vantage point of their absence. In taking a no-salary, zero-income year away from my teaching, I would be acting on a line that touched me personally as well as professionally: "How can a man remember well his ignorance which his growth requires who has so often to use his knowledge?"[5]

I was certain that the willing support of my husband would add more zest to my undertaking than if I were single and accountable only to myself. There is a *withness* of feelings, of strengths and weaknesses, of joys and sorrows, of easiness and struggle, of speaking and silence that only marriage can give us. Many, citing Thoreau's solitude, said that marriage disqualified me from my experiment in voluntary poverty. But aloneness is part of marital togetherness and half the pleasure of being alone in such a relationship comes from being able to *say* how much we enjoy reflection, books and solitude.

It was through teaching Thoreau's *Walden* that I decided to make a year's experiment with uncommitted living. I did not come to such a decision "in blind obedience to a blundering oracle or through a seeming fate commonly called necessity."[6] If my work resembled the twelve labors of Hercules it was simply because it left me no time to do anything else. And the gift I set out to give myself was freedom from the bell-set rigidity of inflexible schedules. How often I had wishes, during a forty-five minute

A WOMAN'S WALDEN

class period, that we could have an entire day to discuss those words that, as Milton said, "are not dead things." What would it matter if we did not "cover the material"? Imagine one entire day devoted to a single academic subject. How much more would be absorbed. What a pioneer effort it would require to take such a path through years of tradition and custom.

What would a day ungoverned by the relentless clock grant me? I knew I would waken to sunrise and I was thankful that the necessities of a schedule had so fastened that to my body rhythms. There would be time to listen to the wind, watch it play with the palm fronds of my three-stringed harp of the winds, my small island of three palm trees. I would linger over each meal; silence or speaking would be more important than any work that needed to be done. Yet the practical tasks of bedmaking, dishwashing, food preparation would fasten me to reality and balance my excursions into the interior self. Physical work could be done without thinking or without the necessity of being absorbed in intellectual work. There would be a simple rhythm to each day, mornings for writing, afternoons for gardening and outdoor walks, evenings for being free to each other's sharing. There would be leisure to watch a sunset in the sky over our pond and its mysterious "double" in the twilight waters.

Meantime the humiliations and stern realities of involuntary poverty haunted me. Remembering my childhood in a series of homes that were somehow never home, I puzzled over my wish to "copy" Thoreau. Did I really want to go back, even for a year, to poverty? It followed that my first step toward Walden III was to question how much I could eliminate of what we of the twentieth century have come to regard as necessities. I decided that the simplified life should be less a place than an experience. We should have as many Waldens with as many variations as there are people. True, I have neighbors next door, yet the inner lives of us all inevitably places us whole continents apart.

In a year of "thumbnail" living, the "delicate handling" I

"Delicate Handling"

purposed to give myself would grant me the time I had long complained of not having. Would such time reveal what I had hidden from myself in the distractions of a many-sided career? Euripides called time a babbler that speaks even when no questions are asked. The accumulated yesterdays that seemed too full will reappear in the meanings they give to this present moment.

Since I would earn no wage I wanted to fracture the idea that time is money. Yet I would cultivate my time more carefully than when it was the "coin" by which I earned my daily bread. Of course my cultivation would not be what we have come to regard as practical. I hope to elevate quiet times alone, to re-possess myself inwardly through thinking, writing, reading, studying and physical work. I want to give my thoughts the room and space they cannot have in bits and snatches "stolen" from a mass of work-related distractions. Perhaps there is a double destiny in these words, "As he thinketh in his heart, so is he."[7]

Chapter 2
"Thumbnail Living"

Simplicity, simplicity, simplicity! I say, let your affairs be as two or three, . . . and keep your accounts on your thumbnail.[1]

To simplify my life I will not drive or ride in a car, will have no phone, no electric lights, no television, no radio, no concerts, no museums, no places of business, no shopping forays, no community demands, no good citizen appeals, no newspapers. In brief, I will have nothing that will lead to the fragmentation that necessity has forced on women. But the multiplicity that confronts a modern woman also confronts the modern man; quite simply, I want to test my own dependence on these things and activities in my life. Because I do not want my experiment to be a trivial or temporary amusement, it must be rather inconveniently long.

What are the basic necessities of life? Food, shelter, clothing and fuel. If self-maintenance is to become a pastime, all my wants will have to be lessened. In eating less, I think of those who scrounge in garbage cans for food and realize that any lasting improvement of their lot can best be effected if we begin with ourselves. When we give money or food we do not permanently relieve poverty. I wonder if our own voluntary poverty would be a means of teaching the poor to manage better with less? Deep down no one wants things to be done *for* them. Perhaps in my experiment I will learn how *little* one can manage with, not how *much*. When I am tempted to add one more dish to my menus, I must remember those for whom not even a dish is available. I *can* choose a simpler diet, a simpler way of life, a "Spartan simplicity" if you please. If the "turnpike road" to most people's hearts is through their stomachs, let me choose to eat so as to live and not, as our landscape dotted with restaurants would seem to indicate, live to eat.

I began with morning coffee. Barley browned carefully in the oven and ground just as coffee is ground produces a brown drink with a nutty, cereal-like flavor. Homebaked bread made with blackstrap molasses, whole wheat flour and coarsened with generous amounts of a cheap bran makes a heavy dark loaf that one could well hide in a straw mattress just as Ivan Denisovitch did in that labor camp in Russia. I like it much better than its snow-white, foam-like counterpart. Molasses-moist I eat thick slices "as is" but with my homemade fruit jams it is—in terms of its nutritional value—food fit for a king.

Such bread nourishes us twice. As we smell it baking, the fragrance carries us back to a simpler age, where the oven door of an old black range was left open after the bread was removed. Mom would draw up her rocking chair and rest her slippered feet on the warm door, surveying with deep satisfaction her eight loaves of freshly baked bread. As we eat such bread we are fed both physically and psychologically. Bread-baking is a poetic process rather than merely culinary and chemical. The action of the yeast is a constant sermon in the triumph of the small and seemingly inconsequential. The touch of human hands turns any creation into God's grandchild because we are extending the chain of descent; God created us so that whatever we create becomes third in creation's line.

What do we have, those of us who think we have something to give? What have we to pass on if it does not begin with what we ourselves have received? Has it not been by receiving that we

"Thumbnail Living"

have learned to give? Unless the poor can share and learn from our poverty, how can we expect our charity to be more than a mere cosmetic, conscience-soothing gesture?

Since I do not carry my house on my back, my little cottage was built for me through an excellent form of barter. In a sense, the labor that supported my body and built my house simultaneously enlarged my mind. This labor was teaching. It is a work that favors women. As a mother I had no other career, and when my children were small I suffered keenly as I envied women who had careers. Not that I wanted to escape from my home and children so much as I wanted the *things* that a career made possible. At the same time I was fiercely possessive of every small change in my little ones. On looking back I am glad that circumstances spared me the necessity of exchanging my little ones for wall-to-wall carpets and such. Had circumstances decreed it, I suppose I could have combined motherhood with a career, and the children might have been the better for it. I refuse to judge those who must work, but if I had to work, what irreplaceable pleasures I would have missed!

My mothering years took nothing away from the development of my mind, even though my children's child-years were years when I did, indeed, "steal" hours for concentrated reading. Meanwhile, the dusting and other housework became the incubation periods for that reading to grow and reach out for a verifying experience on which to test or communicate what I had learned from it.

However, when I maintain that work of the hands coordinates well in the lives of women, I do not speak of women who must do what we have traditionally called a man's work. Such people, whether men or women, must come home from their work *marked* by the trade or profession to which they give the better part of their lives. Those who work as business executives, doctors, lawyers, factory workers, construction workers, miners, teachers or laborers must support themselves with work that denies the mind its full freedom. Shelter or "home" as we commonly call it is, for them, no more than a luxurious foxhole, a burrow, a bedroom, regardless of the number of rooms their shelter boasts. The mortgage they pay is "the amount of what I will call life which is required to be given in exchange for it, immediately or in the long run."[2]

For the woman who works at homemaking tasks, this life of sleep and work has much more variety. Every requirement that goes toward maintaining a home occupies the hands, but leaves the mind free. The daily dusting of furniture does not keep the furniture of our minds undusted unless we neglect the needs of the mind by concentrating on things.

What are the so-called "needs" of the mind? My early teachers were constantly reminding us that we must put the needs of our minds and souls *first* every day of our lives. As the needs of the body had to be met with necessary food, even more necessary were the needs of mind and soul that were housed in the body-temple. If exercise improved the body, they reasoned, then mental exercise dictated that reading should require mental effort. If the mind was to be "fed," something more difficult than "easy reading" was necessary; something that would nibble away at one's thinking while work of the hands went on. "Don't settle for pleasurable reading," they said. "Choose something that requires effort."

As children, we were also compelled to memorize long passages of Scripture and not unexpectedly, we thoroughly disliked it. Years later, when life and experience had proved the truth of such ancient words as "Man is born unto trouble, as the sparks fly upward,"[3] our rote memorization could be said to have rescued us. Suffering took on a common-to-man color that saved us from self-pity. Such remembering has a way of returning at the oddest times with strangely appropriate reminders or helps.

It is not that our furniture requires dusting; it is, instead, a matter of priorities. If the mind is filled with the "food" of ideas

"Thumbnail Living"

first, before housework or any physical work is undertaken, one is hardly aware of the house. Of course, this is also why I have such a "passion" for educating women. In the words of Charlotte Brontë, "Keep your girls' minds narrow and fettered and they will still be a plague and a care, sometimes a disgrace to you. Cultivate them, give them scope and work and they will be your gayest companions in health, your tenderest nurses in sickness, your most faithful prop in old age."[4]

As a further parallel to the modern view of necessities, I decided to discover for myself how well I could manage without a car. People asked what I hoped to accomplish by doing without a car for the period of one year. It is certain I was not setting out to find or influence followers. Friends who felt kindly toward my eccentricities would snicker and say, "I'll give you exactly two weeks." One of them proved correct. So automatic was my attachment to cars that when a friend drove past to show us his new car saying, "Hop in, we'll drive around the block," I automatically slipped into the front seat just as Larry, who had predicted the two weeks, pulled along side of us. Pointing an accusing finger at me, he yelled triumphantly, "What did I tell ya?" Confronted with proof positive of my mindless aquiescence, I hastily jumped out.

That brings me to the matter of clothing. A friend stopped in to ask if she could get me anything at a nearby shopping center, adding, "Just think, you could go along with me, if you didn't have to keep that silly vow of yours." For a minute I envisioned that shopper's paradise with its living trees and its two-storied waterfall, its combination of attractive merchandise and Nature's finest manifestations. There you will hear the music of white water falling over granite rocks, see exotic lush flowers and living trees under a glass sky overhead, with tapes of birds singing. What was missing? Only mountains, desert, seashore and solitude, and the "real" of unplanned nature.

Apart from the aching feet that a shopping expedition may or

A WOMAN'S WALDEN

may not cause, what actual powers would I lose by going? First of all, too many visits to shopping centers produce a subtle distortion within ourselves. Almost without our volition new wants are created, higher (meaning more expensive) standards are mentally visualized and the multiplied varieties of merchandise to which we are exposed make our attachments to what we already possess shallow and unsatisfactory. It is not merely that our possessions have a built-in obsolescence; we contribute to their obsolescence by an insatiable craving for variety. In the process, we ourselves become no longer creators but consumers, no longer givers but takers, no longer free but snared by the lusts of our eyes till our very personalities are reduced to little more than a set of multiplied wants.

What does my refusal amount to? Without my car all distance must be reckoned in terms of my two feet. I am either a biped without feathers or bicyclist. How far do I want or intend to bicycle? Such considerations merely account for physical distance. Words can take me "lands away."

It follows that here I do not have to decide whether to dress "from a love of novelty and a regard for the opinions of men or for genuine usefulness."[5] Having few public functions to attend, usefulness will be my first consideration. People who judge by clothing are not interested in what sort of person the wearer is; they want to know that the wearer of a pair of Gucci shoes has demonstrated his superior intelligence by the fact that he can afford them. The talent for making money is regarded as more important than character. The temptation is to accept what *appears* to be rather than what *is*.

Since fashion decrees that we follow "the head monkey in Paris"[5] I am reminded of the period when garments were made to seem a covering for a plank that gave the human figure the appearance of wearing a sack. Later, we had the high fashion known as "let-it-all-hang-out." I pitied teen-age girls whose innocence was lost in obedience to fashion. Then we had the

"Thumbnail Living"

"poor-boy look." It became fashionable to buy material simulating patches, or pre-bleached fabrics designed to look old and worn. Shabby garments, bearing costly price tags became the "in" thing to wear.

For my experiment I bought nothing new. But I was not denied the pleasure of variety and change. I went to a church rummage sale where used dresses had been carefully sorted and tastefully displayed; there I was able to buy four dresses for twenty-five cents each! Naturally their original purchase price required a higher level of income than my experiment warranted paying. I require of any dress I wear, whether in poverty or prosperity, that I may admire it before I buy it and forget it in the wearing. I hope I am aiming at something higher than fashion as well as something more timeless.

Chapter 3
At a Standstill

There were times when I could not afford to sacrifice the bloom of the present moment to any work, whether of the head or hands. I love broad margins to my life.[1]

Electric lights never seemed a luxury to me until the huge power plant that provided them for New York City broke down. This has happened twice in my lifetime. The blackout that followed one such power failure provoked an orgy of crime and made me wish I could erase from my memory the scenes of animalistic looting, smashing of glass and the mindless intensity on human faces that were brought into our living rooms by the ever-present television cameras. Did I say animalistic? I am insulting the animals to whom a "nature red in tooth and claw" is the norm. Here were people who had been steeped in visual violence from their impressionable infancy, when the mind operates like a computer memory bank, where memories and emotions are stored and replayed in as vivid a form as when they were first seen. Who can measure the cumulative influence of the camera on human morality?

Did Nero fiddle while Rome burned? Here before our eyes millions "fiddled" while Americans marauded, raped, killed, stole and betrayed other Americans.

A decade earlier, in 1966, New York had had its first blackout. Since I was then teaching in the city, I had my students write

A WOMAN'S WALDEN

compositions about their experiences. (How I wish I had kept them.) In every account they described vivid examples of mutual helpfulness, along with feelings of indefinable equality. Their actions tacitly expressed, "Yes, we're all in this together." It, too, was proudly publicized by the media and recorded as a night when less crime than might otherwise be expected took place.

Ironically, there is unanimous agreement that "one picture is worth a thousand words," yet under no condition will such an agreement lead to a prohibition of depictions of violence. History has proved that the pen is often mightier than the sword; will it also prove that pictured violence, along with our human affinity for imitation, is more lethal than atomic bombs? True, atomic bombs are capable of destroying whole cities and perhaps nations, but mass violence to a mass audience, via the eyes, strikes at the roots of the human capacity for goodness.

Thoreau's suggestion that we "try our lives by a thousand simple tests"[2] made me decide to impose a private, self-initiated blackout. It would have been ridiculously easy to turn on a light but to earnestly make an experiment of this sort the period of testing had to be inconveniently long. For three months we used only candlelight and I found I could write or cook—though I could not sew—with no loss of ease or pleasure.

After reading and meditating on a passage from Pascal, I would find myself studying the candle's flame. The oval globe of light from a candle has none of the nervous twitchings of neon but is like a slow ballet of graceful bowing to the invisible currents of air in the room. I was reminded of that Light which darkness cannot comprehend; my candle was a concrete parallel to that truth.

Should not light of any sort be an analogy for spirit? But electric lights have become a mechanical commonplace, an instant daylight, and we accept the masquerade. When I was using electric light I was spurred into doing work-projects far into the night. Technology has lengthened nature's day and

At a Standstill

turned our night hours into an artificial day. There is no denying that we are made outwardly richer by such practices. But, a candle breathes and pulsates with the air around it in a union of light with life, of matter with spirit.

In giving up something so commonplace as electric lights, even in a brief three-month experiment, I had the adventure of seeing my ordinary life in an extraordinary light. In the end I might discover that the Light is not in candles nor incandescent lighting, nor in circumstances, nor in accumulation of things, nor in anything external. The Light must be in my own soul.

On our first night without electric lights we found ourselves in a theater! We had ringside seats at the sunset over our pond. Actually, we had twin sunsets, one in the western sky and another in the dusky mirror of the pond. When the western lights became "a mastery of flame where quick gold lies," and as "the last lights off the black West went," we found ourselves hushed. Those parts of us that were "seared with trade, bleared, smeared with toil,"[3] and wore the stains of commercialism, seemed somehow removed.

A quiet silence followed in which there was a peaceful darkness and stillness; a sense of almost timeless time in which to think deeply of Hopkins' line, "Nature is never spent . . . . Because the Holy Ghost over the bent world broods with warm breast and with ah! bright wings."[4]

Not wishing to alter our sunset Orion, I said, "Let's light just one candle and see how much illumination it gives." At once the room was transformed. The furniture cast shadows on the ceiling and shapes that we never saw by day took on a life of their own. The ordinary took on mystery. The human form seemed to present itself without the intrusion of highlighted wrinkles or fatigue. We found ourselves speaking more slowly and quietly.

Was that merely the calming of a sunset preview before dark? Or was it the "to-fro tender trambeams" of a single candle? It made me wonder if peace is purchased only in stillness. I carry from that companionable silence the sure knowledge that "piecemeal peace is poor peace . . . . When Peace here does house, He comes with work to do, He does not come to coo. He comes to brood and sit."[5]

Chapter 4
Home: Our First Paradise

Man was not made so large limbed and robust but that he must seek to narrow his world, and wall in a space such as fitted him. He was at first bare and out of doors, . . . Adam and Eve wore the bower before other clothes. Man wanted a home, a place of warmth, of comfort, first of physical warmth, then the warmth of the affections . . . .

Every child begins the world again, to some extent and loves to stay outdoors, even in wet and cold. It plays house, as well as horse, having an instinct for it.[1]

Were my most primitive ancestors surviving in me when I played house as a child? Surely something libidinal operates in the little boy who chooses caves and tunnels and the little girl who ties strings around trees and says, "This is the wall of my kitchen, and here is my hall and my living room and bedroom." In both, there is a return to that Edenic garden, the bower. It is not a shelter children look for in their first huts and playhouses; rather, they represent a nest, a home, a yearning for comfort and a "make-believe" life not yet entered upon.

Did I own that first shelter of my child-play because it cost so little? Have I in adulthood replaced it with "a workhouse, a labyrinth without a clue, a museum, an almshouse, a prison or a splendid mausoleum"?[2] I cannot say I have ever possessed a workhouse, since we live in an age of labor-saving devices. (In

A WOMAN'S WALDEN

many instances, it seems, "labor-saving devices" cause more work than they save.)

I once rented a house in Europe that had no refrigerator or icebox. Attached to the kitchen was a log-walled room, measuring nine by twelve feet. The logs had been painted, and I was told that this was the "cold room" where food was kept. I attacked the dirt in the long-vacant room with a large wire-bristled scrubbing brush. When I returned to America, I decided to compare the time it had taken to clean the cold room with the time it would take me to clean my chrome and enamel refrigerator. The latter is designed by men whose only contact with food must take place in their mouths and stomachs. Judging by design, the actual model, as well as the paper specifications, are a paragon of apparent simplicity and utility. "Streamlined" is the word used to describe the lack of bulky appearing corners, etc. I used the word "apparent" since both the simplicity and utility are visual rather than practical. Of course the butter, milk and fruit are kept far colder than my European cold room could keep them in July, but aside from this, I will take the "cold room" any day!

Given the same period of disuse, the refrigerator took much longer to clean. Rubber gaskets around the door seem deliberately designed to catch food particles, for they are fashioned in grooves of three. The decorative chromium on the doors is also finely and closely grooved (how lovely it must have looked on the draftsman's sheet!). It was necessary to find an old toothbrush in order to dislodge food particles that children's fingers had deposited on the grooved chrome. The shining racks inside the box slide out, supposedly for "easy cleaning." But the tracks on which these shelves run are also receptacles for stale odors of mingled foods, and a toothbrush or ordinary brush is useless for cleaning them. A cloth wrapped around the blade of a sharp knife works best. Inside the door are more shelves for eggs, butter, ketchup, mayonnaise, pickles, mustard and the like. If these could be designed without soil-collecting "grooves" the modern woman's

Home: Our First Paradise

appliances could be as speedily cleaned as that primitive cold room where all supplies were placed on unpainted wooden tables or the floor.

Surely the Indian squaw with her crock of grains, her stone mortar and pestle, her smoked meat, was not any more wearied in her household tasks than the modern woman's apprenticeship or slavery to her household appliances, decorated with miniscule washboard surfaces.

Another myth is the fabled convenience of an automatic washer. While standards of personal cleanliness are admittedly more stringent today, the daily change of clothing is not practiced in remote corners of our world. Here, too, I had the fortunate experience of doing the laundry for myself and my three sons on the bank of a small stream. My teacher in the primitive art of washing clothes was a native of the area and volunteered to show me "how we do it over here."

Accordingly, she took a huge black iron pot, a good thirty inches in diameter, and set it on a rock-surrounded hole near the river. When I protested that the pot must be dirty, she spat on her finger and ran it around the inner sides of the pot, then showed me there was not a sign of dirt on her moistened hand. Two apertures, one in front and one in the back of the pot, would be the pit for the fire. First, soap was poured in, then buckets of water from the river were added. Our buckets were galvanized pails to which heavy ropes had been attached, so we could throw them into the river and haul them onto land when they were full. Four buckets of water filled the pot. After making certain the soap was dissolved, we added the sheets, towels, underwear, shirts and lightly soiled colored fabrics. Nothing dark was placed in this water. At that, she said, "Now we will let them soak until tomorrow."

The next day, sticks and twigs were pushed into the forward opening. A fire was started, and from time to time the clothes were stirred with a large, narrowly rounded paddle. When they

A WOMAN'S WALDEN

began to boil we could see the dirty water in the pot. She did not let the clothes boil long, but used her paddle to rinse them in the cold running water of the stream. They were wrung out loosely by a hand wringer and hung on wire lines for the sun to bleach and dry.

When the pot was empty of the white clothes, she put the dungarees, dark shirts and dark socks into the same soapy water. With the fire out and the water cool enough for comfort, she scrubbed these items on a grooved board using the "heel" of her hand, not the knuckles as most of us would assume. These were also rinsed thoroughly in the river.

The entire process took less than two hours, and it would be a full two weeks before we would wash again. In winter it was the custom to wait until spring to do all laundry, except for the daily hand-wash of socks and the like. Hence young girls of this region would begin accumulating their household linens at age thirteen and fourteen. A mature woman told me she had fifty sheets when she married.

Obviously, I am not recommending a return to primitive conditions, but it might be well to consider the future of the automatic washer as we now know it. Perhaps it will require the crusted soil of our dried-out water reservoirs to turn back the clock on our so-called labor-saving devices.

If we judge by the acres and acres of developments that have sprung up across the land, it would seem that the average home buyer exercises very little shrewdness or deliberation in his choice of dwelling. In their thirst for the fastest return on all investments, our huge industrial plants are the labyrinths in which men exchange the hours and days of their lives to pay a twenty- and thirty-year mortgage on a house. Factory workers, in some hour of old-age leisure, tell, with apparent satisfaction, of a crushed hand for which "compensation" gave them nine-hundred dollars and no loss of pay. Or, they will tell of lifetime deafness from the fumes of the chemical works, which provided

Home: Our First Paradise

their life's rate of exchange for a dwelling and actually gave them no more than a place to sleep. The more fortunate live in houses that are miniature museums, filled with valuable art and memorabilia, there just for display, rather than loved associations.

The home becomes a prison when it locks its owner into terms so demanding that he must, just as any sentenced criminal, serve out his term in work he may detest in order to pay his mortgage. Not once, for the duration of such a term, can he call himself a free man.

There are also dwellings common to the twentieth century in which so-called sophisticated people live in what are little more than boxes stacked one upon the other. They are, for all their glass and steel, reminiscent of what an over-grown boy playing with giant-sized blocks would build. They are called high-rise apartments. It is obvious that spatial considerations take precedence over human needs.

Air space is also utilized with squared blocks rising over highways and city streets. Square cubes of soaring steel and cement with box-like rooms allow for no subtle beauty; there is no allowance made for personal tastes or eccentricities. When tenants of these buildings consign themselves to two- and three-year leases, they do so on one main premise: convenience. This is the "core of truth" on which the mass of men base their choice of dwelling. Should "convenience" change, there is an ever-present American slogan that accounts for our social mobility: "We can always move somewhere else!" The pleasures of design, of construction, of furnishing and perhaps of thinking are taken over by others. There is one requirement: convenience. For the sake of convenience men will gladly relinquish their capacities for struggle, for sustained effort, and for self-determination.

What are the results? That which once grew from an inner need, or from poverty if you please, became known as quaint or old-fashioned. People now pay money to stand in long lines to look

A WOMAN'S WALDEN

for a moment on a home where every curved wall, the sloping floors, every common utensil is endowed with an inner beauty. Need determined every choice, and out of this grew the fascination that makes modern man slow down his fast-paced life for a brief look at what he terms primitive and inconvenient.

In acquiring furniture, I began from a position of involuntary poverty. Three functions were to be served: necessity, utility and beauty. Not once, whether in poverty or out of it, have I approached my nesting tasks from the viewpoint of what is fashionable. Was it egotistical to want my home to "look" like me? Could inanimate objects resemble their owners? This belief puts me at odds with certain people, and it occurs to me that in furniture, as in dress, too many have more regard for the dictates of style than for need and usefulness.

My own goal is the fulfillment of a need; along with that, utility and beauty are as necessary as the needs they will satisfy. This is in no way unique. However, I determined that the furnishings of my home should be an outward and visible sign of an inward and spiritual grace.

For me, homemaking is a sacramental calling and home purchases are an expression of the reverence I have for the obligations this involves. Accordingly, they must never be mere acquisitions; to merely acquire would be little more than to lay up treasures on earth. For my purposes, they are vehicles twined round with memories. I have been known to give away family heirlooms because the person to whom they once belonged had an active dislike for me. My best critic, and the one I always want to influence, is the very small child who walks into my house for the first time, and her first shy, yet spontaneous, words are, "Oh, but you have a pretty house!" I would not exchange such praise for the commendation of any interior decorator, no matter how famous.

Chapter 5
"Where I Lived and What I Lived For"

I chose a woman's Walden ". . . because I wished to live deliberately, to front only the essential facts of life, and see if I could not learn what it had to teach, and not, when I came to die, discover that I had not lived. I did not wish to live what was not life, living is so dear; nor did I wish to practice resignation, unless it was quite necessary. I wanted to live deep and suck out all the marrow of life, . . . and if it proved to be mean, why then to get the whole and genuine meanness of it, and publish its meanness to the world; or if it were sublime, to know it by experience, and be able to give a true account of it in my next excursion." [1]

This is, for us, a visual age. In a matter of minutes we are able to consider places as far apart as Australia and Tibet; from our armchairs we need only turn the pages of a magazine or touch the knob of our television sets, and "rising expectations" are set in motion.

Technology and commerce have afflicted us with a national restlessness that has revolutionized every human life. Ours has been called the Age of Change, because more than any other age we have extended not only physical frontiers—space-shots are now almost commonplace—but our social and moral frontiers. An ancient writer said, "They are wise to do evil, but to do good

A WOMAN'S WALDEN

they have no knowledge";[2] there is an increasing gap between our "technological ingenuity" and our ability to *use* and apply that ingenuity to the pace and human interactions of our lives.

But how many years have I allowed to escape me while I, too, have mentally lived in some pristine wilderness or made my escape from modern civilization through the trivial and, perhaps, regressive significance of a return to quiet evenings of candlelight and leisure? Shall I discover that I am ". . . rich in proportion to the number of things I can afford to leave alone?"[3] I do consider myself happier for having been denied the ownership of many a place I once considered buying. I never got my fingers burned by actual possession. My life was not mortgaged to pay for what I now know would have cost twice the initial estimate; hence, I am richer with no loss of time or money.

Some will call this "sour grapes," but sufficient time has elapsed between those mental purchases of mine and the present to bring to my remembrance that multiplied possessions bring multiplied problems. Yet I am certain that I shall always be fascinated by the challenge of changing one's environment.

My disposition inclines toward the unknown and untried. Surely women as well as men share Alexander's fear that there may be no more worlds to conquer, even if that refers only to our own personal little worlds within this world. This is quite opposite from that emphatic statement, "But I would say to all my fellows, once for all, as long as possible live free and uncommitted."[4] It makes little difference if we were committed to property or to jail. For me, this year meant a freedom from my commitment to security.

To attempt even this twentieth-century approximation of voluntary poverty meant that I must give up the salary on which I had grown totally dependent. I found it odd that the first step in the direction of living free was learning I was virtually a slave to financial security.

In order to train myself to live without a paycheck for one year,

"Where I Lived and What I Lived For"

it was necessary while I was still earning money, to begin with self-denial. Purchases that were commensurate with my income had to be sacrificed. Some of my contemporaries regarded this move as unnecessary and unnatural. Personal pleasure, personal indulgence and personal advantage are the criteria for the "good life." To voluntarily renounce things that were legitimately good was looked upon as a result of a martyr complex.

In preparing for this year, I exchanged possessions that were good and reasonable for the possession of a power over myself, the power to follow my convictions in the face of ridicule, the power of dependence on what is invisible and unchanging rather than on the visible and transitory. Furthermore, how could I claim poverty if I did not give myself a single privation? It probably would never have occurred to me if I had not had those years of teaching, as literature, Thoreau's doctrine of simplicity.

The first step to voluntary poverty was to get rid of as many misconceptions as I could while I was earning the income of a middle-class American. In the total sociology of our class structure, perhaps it was not such a big step. A teacher, simply by virtue of the salary he or she makes, is firmly in the lower middle-class. Certainly no one can *know* poverty without experiencing it. It cannot be taught. In fact, I am wondering as I write this whether I can even explain it.

In my mind, one of the most common misconceptions is that there is disgrace in poverty and virtually an automatic respect for those who are rich. Yet one of the privileges of poverty is that one is not anxious of what the world regards as misfortune. When we recognize and yield our love of luxury and our bottomless greed for more, when we are free from hunger and thirst, sheltered against the cold, and we have time to find beauty in Nature, we are truly wealthy. What makes our indigence painful is *our own view of it.* We cannot always conceal our poverty, nor should we try. At the same time, we should resist society's view that poverty is despicable or that it is evil to be poor. We have in

A WOMAN'S WALDEN

reasons modern life is so shallow and superficial. Such dawns know nothing of *renewal*. When our lives are bound by the mechanical and outward, we cannot even make a reflective comment about ourselves because we have never met the renewed "I" that is not the "I" of the coffee cup. In the demands of a paid job and post-morning hours, we are too busy to make our acquaintance with a renewed self, and our modern alienation is not so much an estrangement from others as it is our own alienation from ourselves.

When we are only awake to the world of things and functions, our self-awareness becomes objective, and we know ourselves in the same way that we know objects that are alien to us. Meanwhile, that which should be first in our waking moments—the only thing that can awaken us to a true self-awareness—waits to unseal our eyes. But I had to embrace poverty, that is, give up the exertions of a well-paying job, in order to greet that dawn where my thinking could keep pace with the sun. Here I can experience for myself that "the day is a perpetual morning. It matters not what the clocks say or the attitudes and labors of men."[7]

> *We must learn to reawaken and keep ourselves awake, not by mechanical aids, but by an infinite expectation of the dawn, which does not forsake us in our soundest sleep. I know of no more encouraging fact than the unquestionable ability of man to elevate his life by conscious endeavor . . . . To effect the quality of the day, that is the highest of arts. Every man is tasked to make his life, even in its details, worthy of the contemplation of his most elevated and critical hours.*[8]

Yes, I left the city for a quiet village because I wanted to be out of what we call "the world." I wanted to avoid conformity to convention and immersion in routine. Many wish to "live

"Where I Lived and What I Lived For"

deliberately," even though they may not give voice to it, and those who take steps to change their lives are agreed that they too, do not want to discover at the point of death that either they have not lived, or lived what is not life.

Does life mean money? I pray to be kept from the love of it. I do not ask to be spared the *need* of it; just let me escape the love of it which all too frequently leads to insatiable material cravings. I want to be kept also from the sort of ambition that masquerades as aspiration, remembering that it was through ambition that the rebellious angels fell. I want to be kept from laziness that goes about disguised as activity. We waste lives in multiplied activities rather than take on the struggle that is required to reduce our affairs to "two or three." Regrettably, the laziness that poses as activity is regarded by many as preferable to facing the fewest essentials of life.

To simplify one's life is far more difficult than to resist the thousand and one solicitations with which we are daily bombarded. Simplifying life sets us on a course at odds with the total culture in which we live. What we think of as efficiency may be no more than passive conformity. We prefer to be lost in social subservience than to be known as eccentrics or oddballs. In the crowd we do not risk the need to act on our own. Here we are surrounded by others whose resignation hides under such cliches as, "You can't fight city hall. Why fight 'em? Join 'em!"

In the crowd we can avoid all forms of genuine confrontation. Constant distractions assist us in growing insensitive until we no longer choose our own way. There can be no real dialogue because our immersion is so complete we cannot resist; we let ourselves be pushed. "The only cure for it—is in rigid economy, a stern and more than Spartan simplicity of life and elevation of purpose."[9]

Such a sentence reads as if one could begin by tackling the question of money. In a sense, I did begin there; that is, I planned how I could reduce my wants and needs and do without a salary. You will note I put "want" before "need." When I began to be

A WOMAN'S WALDEN

critical of my own expenditures, I saw that my wants came ahead of my needs in the use of my money. What changed this? That forceful, "Simplify! Simplify! Instead of three meals a day eat but one; instead of a hundred dishes, five; and reduce other things in proportion."[10]

My sense of purpose was undergirded by a willingness to experiment, which became a resolve to search out the ramifications of the simplified life. It seemed a large order for a woman with a family, not because of any biological difference between male and female, but because I could not totally abdicate the variety of functions I saw as mine.

These functions were mine not simply because I am a woman, for I thoroughly agree with Plato that, "no occupation of social life belong to a woman because she is a woman or to a man because he is a man, but capacities are equally distributed in the sexes, and woman should naturally bear her share in all occupations."[11] However, the equal distribution of capacities does not erase a differentiation that, for me, is based on nothing fixed, but on a *phase* of my life.

Whether male or female, we live with and for other people, and not exclusively with or for ourselves. If others are affected by what we are and say and do, our energies must be directed to that which will work for the good of all. Unfortunately, we too often take the concept of the common good as one that negates individuality; I say it *begins* there. Socrates said, "Let him that would move the world, first move himself." Thus the variety of functions I saw as a deterrent became a new assignment. If I simplified my life, would it be my life alone?

"A Spartan simplicity" must by its very emphasis deny that to which human nature is deeply attached—money, possessions, pleasure, power, luxury, reputation. Our culture says, be poor and take your place among those who are considered failures. And to be voluntarily poor suggests that such a course should be undertaken under the auspices of some religious or communal

"Where I Lived and What I Lived For"

organization. St. Francis and others made the vow of poverty understandable and even romantic. Above all, such religious orders made renunciation a highly respectable and noble act. There were rules and guidelines to follow and superiors to direct the novitiate in firmly established traditions. For the individual outside of any institutional authority, the vow of voluntary poverty is a revolutionary step in the sense that it introduces to society a complete change of values. If such a person moves in a circle of ethnically diverse cultures, he poses no threat. But if his friends and associates are what we call straitlaced, solid citizens, then the out-of-step individual will pose a challenge to their rigidity and will endure from them an often ill-concealed hostility.

I am glad it is not necessary to "escape" into institutionally-sanctioned locations in order to simplify my life. It is not even necessary to "take to the woods," though I find that option most appealing. In my personal experiment, simplicity of life transcends all places and becomes an outwardly simplified but inwardly complex experience.

In reducing our affairs and cutting out nonessential details, it would seem we have to compel ourselves to embark on a course that is at once less strenuous and less hurried. Why is it so difficult to do what is essentially easy, as if it were against our best interests? Specifically, how shall we discover that we can do more by doing less? What we evaluate as "more" must be defined on an individual basis, not by what society or a team of efficiency experts decree.

To do less, we must avoid any undertaking that requires haste or hurry. The waste that haste is famed for creating needs our close attention. How many errors in judgment can be traced to a refusal to take time? How much that is rash is due to speed? How many accidents and falls can be traced to hurry? Worst of all, hurry and haste are the archenemies of quiet and calm. If we are to learn this we must turn our backs on ". . . the mud and slush of opinion and prejudice, and tradition, and delusion, and appearance, that alluvion which covers the globe through Paris and London, through New York and Boston and Concord, through church and state, through poetry and philosophy and religion, till we come to a hard bottom and rocks in place, which we can call reality."[12]

If our first and best guide for finding reality is Nature, then her seasons are discovered in their silent comings and goings. How great is our human need for silence! Are we ourselves not taken from the stony dust of earth? How much we need that stillness, without which it is impossible to become aware of the movement of unseen powers. Neither reality nor peace can be arrived at by our own efforts. There are no technical steps by which another can guide us through formulas or "how-to" arguments.

Our own search for a personal reality and a personal peace have been described as a kind of hunger, a wordless longing that may take years to recognize in ourselves. Paradoxically, we see it quite easily in others and most easily in all of international affairs. On the world level, peace is easily argued from park benches and uneasily approached by heads of state. But world peace will never be achieved by government until it is sought by the "little" people, until they pursue it for themselves, until unrelated, even non-communicating, individuals wrestle with their own peace-destroying involvements. We cannot attain world peace until everyone is willing to work for it.

Personally, I must be willing to renounce that which enables modern man to survive; I must renounce the system that honors and misnames multiplicity as efficiency and my own dependence on society and social approval. This approval, after all, is no more than a fickle bombardment of changing opinions, more and varying interpretations from which I, thinking that dependence was a sign of mature adaptability, have too often carved my own identity. To give it all up is not easy, because it means giving up much more than my dependence and my vaunted flexibility. My

"Where I Lived and What I Lived For"

personal search for peace will be futile if I keep even a small corner of resentment toward others. Rather than admit it is we ourselves who keep peace from our lives, we pretend it is the world, or society, or our mates, or our families.

Again, we hail self-direction and autonomy as answers to our search for peace because we like to give it the definition of freedom and liberty. But peace is not freedom. Real peace is not a human concept; as it is, peace has as many labels as there are individual interpretations for the term. Will history one day regard what we call the "cold war" as an era of peace?

In our churches, we hear without hearing, ". . . the peace of God . . . shall keep your hearts and minds . . ."[13] and I accept the fact that anything less would be a "piecemeal peace." Any peace that my own heart and mind could conjure up would be as fluctuating as my heart's desires and as contradictory as the changing dictates of my mind. Why? Because the human organism cannot divorce itself from the situational contagion of human interaction, economics or politics. What is meant, then, by being kept by something as nebulous as the "peace of God"? Indeed, it cannot be known apart from stillness. As the Psalmist said, "Be still and know that [He is] God."[14]

Does it follow that God will be known in the same manner as we know the sum of two numbers? No. God will be known in the same way that the ancients described sex. "And Adam knew his wife and she conceived a son."[15] We will know God in the life of our bodies and emotions as well as with our mind. "Heart and mind" will know, that is, *experience*, God.

What will be conceived if we gain knowledge of God through stillness? The first offspring of such a knowing or union is love. Does a child resemble its parents, its relatives? A relationship with God, however undefinable you find your encounter, will bring forth love. The second offspring is always joy; the nature of love decrees it. If it is not present in your life, the birth of love was abortive. In the realm of spiritual truths love is always the trademark, and love by its nature brings forth joy. These two are followed by peace.

Begotten of love and joy, the peace of God is nothing less than the evidence of restored harmony, tranquility built on stillness. Apart from stillness there can be no actual apprehension of God. No external force, no human being, can do more than speak to us of and about God. Any true knowledge of God must reach us from within by God, and its first evidence is love.

Chapter 6
Reading

A man, any man, will go considerably out of his way to pick up a silver dollar: but here are golden words which the wisest men of antiquity have uttered, and whose worth the wise of every succeeding age have assured us of;—and yet we learn to read only as far as Easy Reading, the primers and class-books, and when we leave school, the "Little Reading," and story books, which are for boys and beginners; and our reading, our conversation and thinking, are all on a very low level, worthy only of pygmies and manikins.[1]

Whether by electric light or living light, reading, if it is to fulfill its function, must be done first thing in the morning. What is a book's function, you may ask, and why morning? A book must serve the same use as that morning in which I was born, the same utility as the first sunrise, the same service as that first springtime of my life. In brief, a book's function is *renewal*. I want to be born again each morning. I want to recover the wisdom that was mine at birth. I believe that except I become as a little child, I shall lose this daily renewal. Indeed, if truth could be given form from all the pages whereon it is recorded, we would have to agree that it is perennially young, that truth has no past, present or future, because it is timeless. Nevertheless, truth brings all the miracle and glory of a newborn child.

A WOMAN'S WALDEN

I agree that there is no danger of dissipation or luxuriousness in devoting my morning hours to the heroic books, the classics. I did this even when my children were babies. Consequently, in the estimation of other mothers who placed housework first, my rating was low. Meantime, I knew I could iron at midnight with half a mind, but unlike end-of-the-day reading, which lulls one to sleep, I found I had to stretch every faculty I possess in order to internalize even a fraction of the classics' life-changing truths. Of course I read fairy tales to my children as well. (Judging from their adult reading habits, I have learned that very little in life is taught; it is caught. They are all readers.)

"To read true books in a true spirit, is a noble exercise, and one that will task the reader more than any exercise which the customs of the day esteem. It requires a training such as the athletes underwent, the steady intention almost of the whole life to this object. Books must be read as deliberately and reservedly as they were written."[2] For this reason, I feel comfortable with the fact that I read the classics slowly.

They were not written for this age of speed and pseudo-efficiency. In fact, I have begun memorizing five lines a day from Monday through Thursday during my sunrise walk, allowing three subsequent days for review and reinforcement. I am not doing this to serve "a paltry convenience," nor to meet some course requirement, nor to earn more money, nor to gain admiration. Let who will try it for themselves and at their own peril, for it is perilous. No, I am memorizing the classics for purely selfish reasons. "A written word is the choicest of all relics. It is the work of art nearest to life itself . . . carved out of the breath of life itself."[3]

If Alexander could carry the *Iliad* with him in a precious casket, and the Israelites could carry their Ark of the Covenant in advance of all their hosts, I feel the need for these same fortifications that ancient truths can give me. To illustrate:

Reading

> *When you pass through the waters*
> *I will be with you;*
> *And through the rivers, they shall not overflow you.*
> *When you walk through the fire,*
> *You shall not be burned,*
> *Neither shall the flame kindle upon you.*
> *. . . . I will bring the blind by ways they knew not,*
> *I will lead them in paths that they have not known.*
> *I will make darkness light before them*
> *And crooked things straight,*
> *These things will I do for them and not forsake them.*[4]

When I repeat such lines from memory, I am surrounding myself with an antique but powerful armor that is exactly suited to my personal needs. Such words contain what is immortal and timeless in the life of the writer. They are unutterable truths, yet here I find them uttered. There are questions that confound and disturb me. I am curious about what rivers I shall be called upon to cross, what flames I shall risk, what blindness will be made light for me, and wise old Isaiah shows me that he was concerned about these very same things.

No, I will not read "only as far as Easy Reading"[5] takes me. That would be to let myself "read" a thousand words in a single picture by way of television. While I am visually imbibing thousands upon thousands upon thousands of word-pictures, a part of my mind is being atrophied. The picture-making portion of my brain lies passive and unused.

While I am being literally deluged by pictures, a more subtle metamorphosis is taking place. In the space of a short station break, I may be subjected to several commercials. In these, my health, my love life, my transportation needs, my aging processes, my family, and a host of other "needs" are the focus of products presented to stimulate all three levels of my humanity: body, mind and spirit. All faculties are appealed to in order that we

A WOMAN'S WALDEN

should regress to the level of ape-like imitation. But while the desired behavior takes place, and products are usually unquestioningly purchased, the speedy bombardment of stimuli has stripped even the desired purchases of their desirability. We are robbed of the capacity to care deeply for anything because we have allowed our perceptions to be dulled and blunted.

Nowhere is this reading of pictures more damaging than in the young, who are being *conditioned to have no depth of feeling in any area.* The inner drive or force that would allow the living human to grow to self-sufficiency is stifled by the frequency and impact of easy "picture" reading. If this is done from early childhood, the personality will be ruled by externals and robbed of the capacity to choose.

But the greatest loss that comes as a result of a steady diet of picture-reading is in the development of the understanding heart. By understanding, I do not mean merely the ability to explain cause and effect but the acquirement of a broad comprehension of moral, as well as intellectual, knowledge. Habitual television viewing keeps the reader on one plateau where no discrimination need take place, where no standards are raised and where influence is leveled at the lowest common denominator, namely, mass appeal.

From constant exposure to television, the ordinary viewer vegetates and allows the quick succession of imagery to wash over him. Cataclysmic events are related with a frequency that allows for no absorption. Thus we are denied what difficult reading forces us to do: time to pause, reflect and think. As for our feelings, which are our chief instruments for a genuine understanding, the sheer volume and multiplicity of the stimuli to which they are exposed numbs and finally deadens emotional responses. We are turned into vacuous receivers, robbed even of the inclination to sort out a single truth from the avalanche of sensationalism that survives only because it is commercially profitable and satisfies a vulgarized public taste.

Reading

We rarely undertake the complicated process of relating our reading to our lives and acquiring from reading a useful tool by which we can compare, discriminate and judge. Yet verification and vindication for the complexities of living can only be gained from the kind of reading that taxes all our faculties and all our energies. My students are quick to reject reading in this "high sense" and tell me they prefer the maxim, "Experience is the best teacher." I wish that they were acquainted with another, more realistic maxim: "Experience keeps a dear school, but fools will learn in no other."

The narrow range of questions raised by their youthful lives is never expanded by exposure, except to that which is near and immediate, to their own peers and passing passions. "Caught in that sensual music," as Yeats expresses it, perspective and true self-identity are denied them. However sophisticated their lives may appear on the surface, they are internally constricted by the intensity of their youthful emotions, which, because the only information they have comes from their peers, find no solution or outlet. And from their own kind they find no more than echoes and reflections of equally superficial entanglements.

The archetypal presentation of sensuality in the symbols and metaphors of classic literature is so potent that a few sentences can lay bare a psychic wound and provide in the reader's ruminations a wholesome, if vicarious, catharsis. More, it can provide the necessary "distancing" without which there can be no healthy emotional perspective or identity.

As for that "memorable interval" between the spoken and the written words, the orator who tickles my ears often does no more than that, leaving me very little to weigh and consider. Unfortunately, most listeners are beguiled by eloquence, just as they are moved to actions by impulse; thinking does not enter into either pursuit. It is an almost involuntary yielding to the immediate situation.

The truest eloquence is often mute, whereas spoken eloquence

A WOMAN'S WALDEN

is made up of a kind of vehement fire that kindles lesser fires by a contagion of forcefulness. Flamboyant eloquence is often accompanied by gestures, vocal intonations and charismatic charm, but when the same words that move us by tone of voice and intensity are transcribed to writing we find our pleasure was due to the manner of speaking, the time, and the environment of the occasion, rather than to the content of the words. Saddest of all are the actions inspired by mere rhetoric; those who are spurred to act in response to oratory must subsequently search in vain for some lasting conviction in themselves when the occasion is past. Nowhere is this more common than in political rantings or sawdust trail conversions. Politicians have conquered kingdoms with their tongues but not for long. Later, an unadorned idea on a simple piece of paper proves the transiency of rhetoric and the timelessness of truth. Just so the true convert can only find the bedrock of enduring persuasion in the Word made flesh, as silent and imperceptible as life itself.

Chapter 7
Leisure

To affect the quality of the day, that is the highest of arts. Every man is tasked to make his life, even in its details, worthy of the contemplation of his most elevated and critical hour.[1]

My favorite manuscript is written in very large print. Its author intends it to be so large "that he who runs may read." In my early childhood, Nature was my first book. The letters of its pages were so immense, my first wish was to reach out and touch them. When I saw how impossible it was to stretch that far, I realized my own littleness. The consciousness of an infinite power was born in me at that moment. I remember turning a kitten on its back so it could look at my "book" with me, but it wriggled to turn its head downward again. It had no wish to "read" my sky.

In my looking upward, I had many a fall and was often told, "Why don't you look where you are going?" I never dared to reply, "That is what I *am* doing." Nor could I ever believe that that was why I fell.

No, there was no speech or language where the voice of day unto day could not be heard. However, the large print of the universe had its greatest variety in the land of my birth, Norway. It was as if the fingers of God had been very busy fashioning a diversity that would try the ingenuity of its children to the limit. The way in which light and darkness are set one against the other

A WOMAN'S WALDEN

gives a special intensity to the words, "Thou makest the outgoings of the morning and evening to rejoice."[2] It is as if He were granting the inhabitants of that land a special gratification for the strength of each day's declarations. In that land the light of the sun does, in a special manner, declare the glory of God. Depending on the mind-set of the viewer, it has been called the land of the long, long night, or the land of the midnight sun. For me, it is the land of the long, long day.

But when I was a child and read my book of day and night, the sun and stars, was such reading to be put away when I took on the burden and heat of the day? I changed. Did my book of nature change with me? Yes. I saw with sorrow that my eyes, like those of the animals, were turned downward rather than upward in periods when the cares of life crowded out all but a bell-set rigidity of daily requirements. I was, as Hopkins says it, "seared with trade," and the face of all nature changed. I found myself "care-coiled and care-killed." In daily living, I could not resolve my conflicts as the poet did, "Give beauty back . . . back to God, beauty's self and beauty's giver."[3]

"I saw that I could not afford to sacrifice the bloom of the present moment to any work, whether of the head or hands. I love broad margins to my day. At first I tried to set broad margins by adding more hours to the ticking of life's clock and an already overcrowded day. By multiplication or addition, I too would understand what the Orientals meant by contemplation and the forsaking of works."[4] But my days continued to wear the stamp and rule of pagan deities, Woden and hammer-wielding Thor. All days and all time were crowded into activity-tight segments.

Perhaps I hunted too eagerly for that child-beheld beauty? As Emerson said, "Go forth and find it and it is gone; 'tis only a mirage as you look from the window of diligence."[5] Was it my persistent exertion that prevented me from retaining that early harmony with nature? Did the painter, Corot, pray, "Grant that I may see with the eyes of a little child," because he understood that

Leisure

Nature's beauty speaks when it is *unsought* and comes *because* it is unsought.

Is contemplation a denial of its synonym, "reflection," when it is pursued for utilitarian ends? The wide margins of life, like the margins of a page, must be dictated by life's total contents. In a sense, this experiment of mine is like a page from an ancient illuminated manuscript. Here, there is no subordination of parts to the whole, yet the thoughts that wander through that tangle of convoluted colors and lines lead on to the center of the page where small script, or small captive designs, dominate by being central.

To accomplish this on the pages of day-to-day living, I would need leisure, or free time. I did not yearn for idleness; rather, my free time had to be the condition in which I would find leisure. I did not intend for it to be simply absence of work or a negative pursuit. To use my leisure well; to sit and watch the blue heron, the gulls and ducks in the pond; to see the sun turn gray water into silver crescents; to listen to the quiet sound of that same water as it laps against the shore; to smell the mingled odors of the wind after it has passed through the cypress branches; these are the non-utilitarian uses to which I would turn my leisure. It would be my purpose to give my free time to a heightened awareness of common things.

This morning I watched a crystal thread of an egg white as I broke the shell and dropped one lesser sun into a bowl, thinking what analogous forms that sun has granted to itself. Like the clouds surrounding the sun, the albumin surrounds the yellow yolk. Then there are the sun-round oranges, yellow grapefruit, and "to-fro" petals of round daisies and dandelions, all microcosms of the day's sun. Each holds a miniature hint of a greater glory.

But has our work ethic and our preoccupation with efficiency caused us to demand a similar industry and energetic effectiveness from our free time? When we move from work to recreation, do we merely exchange one strenuous role for another and call it

A WOMAN'S WALDEN

play? Women will expend more energy on the tennis courts or in the exercise salons than they will in the care and cleaning of their homes, but they will label their sports "play" and that which actually requires less energy is labeled drudgery. Repetition is characteristic of both pursuits. In neither pursuit is the exertion a once-for-all activity. The only difference is in the attitude of anticipation that precedes play and the reluctance that precedes housework. One has only to enter a house where the achievement of cleanliness and beauty are looked upon as sacred callings, and you will know that even paint and furnishings have a property that can verily be called spiritual. In them the most trivial task takes on an aura that is at once elevating because each *act* is preceded by a loving thought; thus *the act is thought made visible.*

Is it possible that we avoid leisure because it is the "mother of thought"? If so, we must ask if thinking is so tyrannical that we must crowd every day with busy-ness, whether in work or recreation, *in order to avoid thought.* Sleepless people often complain, "I can't turn off my thoughts." They seem hardly aware that by this admission they are confessing to the existence of an oppressive master. But when daily life is spent in an escape from thinking, in activities whose thought requirements lie outside of self, that which is fundamental to our beings must make its bid for attention. "As [a man] thinketh in his heart, so is he."[6] Deny personal thinking by fragmented days, by commerce, by too much social involvement, by noise, by excitement, by a desire for unceasing motion, by continuous achievement, by ambitious projects, and, as long as the physical self remains strong, the interiorization that is thinking may be held at bay. Soon the individual resembles his own fragmented life style; he cannot know wholeness because he is ruled by disunity. Tragically, he may come to prefer it.

It is true that the world of business is full of enterprise, "is unexpectedly confident and serene, alert, and adventurous, and unwearied."[7] Why? Because machinery, lumber, nuts and bolts, wheat, corn, potatoes, barley, bales of hay or bales of rags, carloads of liquor are not sentient. Does iron slumber? In the arenas of commerce, man, who is "the tool of his tools" requires sleep, and if he would have his thoughts covered over like a cloak he must give some of his waking hours to thinking, to the very thoughts he thinks he has escaped in the business world.

In the orbit of our own lives, we should not always be sending our thoughts outward like meteors; there must be a returning course in which our thoughts make their revolutions back to their own source and center of attraction. If leisure is crowded out of life, that hour in which the "ravel'd sleeve of care" is gathered up in sleep becomes, instead, very much like the hour of death.

Sir Thomas Browne said, "Sleep is so like death, that I dare not trust myself to it without prayer." When that unforced leisure that precedes sleep is upon us, it is well if we can turn thoughts that cannot be turned off into periods of consecrated sleeplessness. In the silence of a sleepless night, the troubling thought can be replaced with thoughts that bring peace. When our tiredness and exhaustion hold our thoughts captive and grant us no escape, the oral reading of someone else's prayer lends a palpable truth to the words, "He giveth His beloved sleep."[8] Whose prayer can do this for us? Mere human words can lull me with their dullness or skim too lightly above my troubled thoughts. Only in the Psalms do I find rest; there I can lie down as one who is at home. Why? Because they never fail to lead me to One who was "numbered with the transgressors,"[9] yet was brought from humiliation and the defeat of a cross to the resurrection.

Ideas and words are not enough for me unless they are inextricably tied to something I can also love, something more than thinking new thoughts, much more than a mental support is my need, since I cannot love abstractions. Ideas and words must intertwine with a Truth for which I could live or die. Such Truth leads me to Christ, the Truth made flesh, made in the likeness of

A WOMAN'S WALDEN

men. It follows that my sleeplessness is transformed when it leads me to prayer. At the same time, the impulse to pray does not come from myself. We are drawn to seek God because He draws us, and we cannot so much as turn toward Him unless we had not already been found by Him.

Chapter 8
Socializing

> *Individuals, like nations, must have suitable broad and natural boundaries, even a considerable neutral ground between them . . . . If we speak reservedly and thoughtfully, we want to be farther apart, that all animal heat and moisture may have a chance to evaporate.*[1]

Shall we choose for our socializing only those with whom we are so close that we would name our children for them? And if so, who are these people? Are they not those to whom we gravitate early in our lives when we are most "open" to new acquaintances and new experiences? Such friends were not purchased by gifts but by a mutual delight in each other's presence. We had no need for compliments; our searching each other out was tacitly recognized as the highest compliment. Our mutual imperfections were taken in the same stride with which we endured our own faults; we loved ourselves in spite of them. We wanted no more from each other than to love and be loved. Because such friendships have no end in view, they do not end.

But most frequently, we meet and part "without being aware that we have come very near one another."[2] A more succinct statement of social etiquette would be hard to find, for it implies the truth of an old cliché: "Keep your distance; familiarity breeds contempt." The usages of polite society have made us fearful of

A WOMAN'S WALDEN

intimacy. Perhaps one of the commonest indications of this takes place in gatherings where loud talking is fostered and induced by the continual presence of that mechanical umpire known as "background music."

The need to shout in order to be heard implies a contempt for the exchange of serious thought, as well as a scorn for the undivided attention which good music deserves. Happily, music that demands the whole of one's attention is rarely used as background music, but on occasion Bach and Beethoven are metaphorically burned at the stake over charcoal. Clearly Cerberus invisibly presides at such functions, for body, mind, and spirit are implicitly invited to go away hungry.

On the other hand, is the music intended to maintain a buffer zone of neutrality? If such is the real function of background music at social gatherings, the neutrality might better be interpreted as an indication of the indifference that lies at the heart of most socializing.

Again, the underlying purpose of background music may be for the purpose of driving people closer together physically. By forcing them to shout in order to be heard, topics of conversation are kept "safely" shallow and inane. The need for "neutral ground" between individuals is such that, "if we speak reservedly and thoughtfully, we want to be further apart, that all animal heat may have a chance to evaporate."[3] That remains true for any age.

Unfortunately, socializing in this century has become a highly fragmented pursuit. For too many, friendship has become about as durable as disposable tissues. Involvement may well be total, where even casual acquaintances try out the "one-flesh" intimacy of the sex act, but it is a cheap totality based on brevity. The lemming-like Fort Lauderdale migration is by no means limited to college-age people. Nor do human relations based on brevity necessarily exclude total involvement.

Speed has also invaded all areas of personal interaction. Far

Socializing

less time is required for intimacy to develop than where tradition demanded formality as well as romantic roadblocks to the culmination of intimacy. We mistakenly assume that the whole personality does not relate under conditions of transience, but this is not true. What *is* sadly true is the apparently "throw-away" features of these short, yet total, involvements. They occupy merely one segment of a life-period and are rarely, if ever, carried over for the duration of a lifetime.

Such successive intimacies, periodically discarded, lead to a deadening of one's emotional capacity to care deeply for anyone, for to care deeply and retain the capacity for caring requires that we *deliberately* cultivate long-term commitments. We *can* keep our contacts from being sporadic. It need not be true, as has been said, "You just can't keep up." You can.

True, you cannot keep a close contact with an ever-increasing number of acquaintances, but it is possible to keep commitments to a small number of close friends throughout one's lifetime. Nor will such commitments need to be changed by the fact that one may find his life highly mobile and his range of interests far wider than that of an old friend. If the ability "not only to make ties, but to break them, not only to affiliate, but to disaffiliate, is a highly adaptive skill,"[4] adaptation ought to operate in the areas of life-loyalties as well as in industry.

Adaptable persons should be able to adapt to friends of earlier years, whose lives may or may not have kept pace with their own. Their own widened interests, aptitudes, and/or social class need not be a deterrent to the old-fashioned grace of loyalty and affection. We know that technical knowledge grows obsolete, and prophecies are fulfilled and pass away. But love never changes. If mindless salmon can fight their way upstream against heavy currents, we ought to be able to resist the social current that suggests we must be careful to find "just the right friends." If those friends we now possess do not share our interests, our areas of diversity or specialization, our aptitudes, our professions, or our leisure pursuits, loyalty need not be abandoned for an "optimum" rate of turnover in friendships. We do not have to yield to trends; we *can* resist!

Chapter 9
Guests

What sort of space is that which separates a man from his fellows and makes him solitary? I have found that no exertion of the legs can bring two minds much nearer to one another. What do we want most to dwell near to? Not to many men surely, the depot, the post-office, the bar-room, the meeting house, the school-house, the grocery, Beacon Hill, or the Five Points, where most men congregate, but to the perennial source of our life, whence in all our experience we have found that to issue, as the willow stands near the water and sends out its roots in that direction. This will vary with different natures, but this is the place where the wise man will dig his cellar.[1]

It strikes some people as odd that my husband is my "guest" in this experiment. In a world where marriage is regarded as an "end," and where husbands and wives either terminate their marriages or grow so "familiar" that all elements of surprise are lost, this experiment has retained all the "death-do-us-part" dictates of an earlier age, with the fresh experience, within a bond of unity, of a wide divergence of interests.

In what sense can a husband be a guest? As a retired man, my husband has willingly consented to share an experiment that was never his aim or purpose; in that sense he is a true visitor. This life of voluntary simplicity need not cause him the deprivations that

A WOMAN'S WALDEN

I have deliberately set out to experience. Though we share bed and board, this experiment remains unrelated to his way of life, although the leisure of retirement makes such a diversity possible. Moreover, we are implicitly rejecting that scholarly definition of a durable marriage described as "two mature people with presumably well-matched interests, and complementary psychological needs, and with a sense of being at comparable stages of personality development."[2]

For the first criterion, we do *not* have "well-matched interests." Our interests are totally opposite. What we *do* have is the capacity to be each deeply involved in our own interests, with the ability to detach and share a firm respect for the other's right to completely divergent aims or interests. There is no need for either of us to repress or "play it safe" due to inherent possibilities in the other's pursuits or talents. We can afford to invest the full range of our energies in the pursuit of different, yet united, goals. This poses no threat to either of us because our commitment to each other is based on our previous commitment to endurance. This leaves us free to "afford" a wide variety of experiences.

Of course there are risks, and there are frequent crises of change. But our commitment to the endurance of our marriage is based on something beyond ourselves, which make the rewards greater than the risks. It could be called "creative collaboration." In brief, our marriage does not endure because of any *externals;* our very different personalities have evolved from *within.*

Do we have "complementary psychological needs"? No, we walk to the music of different drummers, but we have the common sense to want with our whole hearts the shared experiences that enduring marriage builds upon. While our strong points and our weak points differ, and where awareness in certain areas turns to oblivion in others, we are secure enough to accept oblivion as an imbalance that is innate rather than meanly intentional.

Are we at comparable stages of personality development? No.

Guests

Does a rose blossom at the same time as lily of the valley? In our case, age differences places us a decade apart. Again, being out of step is no threat because each of us has learned that our full-time respective role, in marriage or out of it, is to be ourselves. Our marriage is, therefore, not according to the above "standard." It is on the side of individuality, which is not always easy to come by, but which neither of us fears.

Thus, instead of encountering a vacuum at the end of his occupational life, my husband is an interested, active observer in an experiment that provides novelty within the framework of a solid marriage. Ours is a freedom to share and explore what is at once predictable and non-predictable in the dictates of what I have set about to examine experientially. Together, we are testing our powers for adapting to change. No bridges have been burned, which leaves us the extraordinary opportunity of deciding which of several futures we shall serve for ourselves.

During our experiment we have had as many as fifty guests at one time in this little house. The usual comment to this news is, "Where did you put them?" Anyone looking at the house would say it is too small for such a group. But I love that old cliché: "Where there is heart-room, there is always house-room." The second question usually put to me is, "What did you serve?"

Before I answer either question, I must admit I never planned to have company in such numbers. It was necessary to borrow chairs and seat at least ten or twelve of the children on the floor. I served carrot sticks and cookies, along with an inexpensive punch that I call "kickapoo" juice, since it lacked all "kick" in the form of carbonated drinks or fermentation. In contrast to what was usually served at such functions, my refreshments were decidedly austere.

It was hospitality for reasons other than hospitality. Like myself, my guests were a group of uprooted people from many different states, backgrounds, and age levels. Their

A WOMAN'S WALDEN

unfinished church building made house meetings necessary. (I know that such meetings were common during the early days of Christianity.)

After construction of the church building I was able to take note of certain differences in human interaction. Had it been the crowded space that initiated the informality? After the formalities of a clergy-directed service in the home, they broke up into twos and threes mingling and intermingling, with the most personal of problems being shared. Under the distancing that took place in the larger surroundings of the new church, I saw that, despite the similarity of purpose and subject matter, the home meeting fostered more spontaneity and emotional warmth in which a little loneliness was lifted. On the other hand, there was a formality and rigidity evident in the spacious church.

Is this why there are dwindling congregations in many of our churches? Is the great upsurge in cell groups and sub-cults of quasi-religious persuasions granting lonely people a greater sense of identity and belonging? Should religion pay greater heed to social interaction among its adherents?

Certainly religious leaders should see that smaller groups demand and receive more total involvement, and an absence of commitment is evident in a large auditorium where religious conversion is equated with a crowd-induced walk to the speaker's platform. This is no more than undifferentiated conformity, quite unlike the life-changing permanence of decisions and inner convictions, made during times of meditation or the one-to-one meeting of St. Paul with his Master.

Saddest of all is the growing absence of professional people from the ranks of organized religion. Because of the millions of dollars being spent on mass appeal, in which every skill and advance in technology is brought to bear in spreading the gospel, millions of people are turned off. Why? Because the dynamic of social responsibility and self-denial, laid down by Christ, has given way to superficial claims that promise, but don't deliver, an instantaneous change in lifestyles. The word used in several English translations of Isaiah's book is "fast," for which I have substituted the word "practice." "Behold, you fast [practice your religion] for strife and debate   Is not this the fast [practice] that I have chosen? to loose the bands of wickedness, to undo the heavy burdens, and to let the oppressed go free, and that ye break every yoke? Is it not to deal thy bread to the hungry, and that thou bring the poor that are cast out to thy house? when thou seest the naked, that you cover him; and that thou hide not thy self from thine own flesh? Then shall thy light break forth as the morning, and thine health shall spring forth speedily: and thy righteousness shall go before you; the glory of the LORD shall be thy reward."[3]

Too many non-churchgoers are saying, and rightly so, "I fear that religion is now big business." Like big business, which would keep us forever a consumer society, religious leaders should beware of practices that propagate mere conformity and dependence to a degree that their followers are "never educated to the degree of consciousness, but only to the degree of trust and reverence, and a child is not made a man, but kept a child."[4]

Let parishioners be asked, along with your "Homeric or Paphlagonian man," whether they have any new ideas. Invariably, a quotation or work-related answer, will be the standard response. Or ask, "Are you always satisfied with yourself? . . . Wishing to suggest a substitute within him for the priest without, and some higher motive for living."[5] It will be found that while such people reverence honesty and all the moral virtues, their highest views are "a simple expediency." One longs to give them Louis Untermeyer's line, "From sleek contentment keep me free."[6]

Unlike an isolated cabin, my house does not give travelers an excuse to stop and ask for a glass of water. Yet many stop because they cannot call me up. I do not have a telephone. Nor can I say I do not miss it. Not that I miss the "invasions of privacy" that my

A WOMAN'S WALDEN

listed phone number brings me; I do not regret being relieved of having to say to solicitors, "How much of your donations go to actual help, and how much to administration?" Never once have I had an answer to that question. One wonders how much money is deflected from government taxes by this time-wasting practice. Clearly, the practice makes money since it is thriving and lustily ringing at mealtimes in too many homes. What I do miss is the sound of a beloved voice. In many instances, when it comes to family communications, phone calls have replaced the letter.

A special guest, a little girl, who thought herself unnoticed as she filled her napkin with cookies, hid her treasures behind her back and said with heart-breaking simplicity, "I wish *we* had a pretty house like yours!" Filling a box with take-home cookies and ignoring her uncombed hair and soiled dress, I hope I planted the seeds of a resolve in her wish as I replied, "Someday, when you are a big lady like me, you will." I also had visits from those whose main appeal was manipulative. They did not seek my hospitality so much as what one has termed my "hospital-ality," people who saw my work as non-work, and my time as too rightly theirs to use in ways they themselves would not want to be used. Fortunately, I did not have many such guests.

Being a woman, though not necessarily *because* I am a woman, I set about to entertain guests at festive dinners with the frank admission that I would serve them for as little money as possible and still provide the atmosphere of an important banquet. The ceremony of a beautiful table setting and the ritual of making certain events memorable through entertainment in one's home is as near to the "communion of saints" as one can get.

It was written of Christ that "He was made known of them in breaking of bread."[7] And how little we know one another apart from what we learn at a shared meal. What togetherness it fosters! But too often we have instead, the television tray in which each member of the family eats with eyes hypnotically riveted to

Guests

the television screen, and mastication is mindlessly matched with whatever the pace of the picture demands.

I did not worry about being rebuffed when I invited my affluent guests to share what I deliberately planned to be a poverty meal. Yet not for a moment did I let myself forget that it is one thing to serve a "cheap" meal with intention, and quite another to serve such a meal because one is forced by an inflexible income to shop with eyes closed to what the affluent are accustomed to buy without so much as a glance at price tags. When I thought of the truly hungry of this world, I breathed a silent apology, because my feast included so many more dishes than their daily bowl of thin rice.

Since so many people have asked me about my "poverty meals" for guests, I kept all the receipts of my experiment in voluntary poverty. In an age when prices change almost daily and the worry and concern of mothers of growing children very often centers around that deep need to provide for them, I can also remember asking, "Will the groceries last until the next payday?" And what if no payday arrives? "Will the unemployment benefits match the appetites of my little ones?" Accordingly, it seems wise to record prices that will probably be obsolete when this book reaches print.

Menu:
Company dinner for ten people:
Stuffed peppers (meat, $2.11, extended with grits)
Potato dumplings (very filling)
Gelatin cucumber salad (homegrown)
Gelatin cranberry salad (one can, plus one apple, plus two sticks of celery)
Carrot sticks (homegrown)
Dessert: From "scratch" economy, buttermilk chocolate cake

Leftovers: four meals for two people!

A WOMAN'S WALDEN

Monthly income: $328.00
Monthly expenditures:
  Tithe: $35.00
  Mortgage: $154.00
  Water: $12.25
  Electricity: $27.10
  Pyro-Fax Gas (cooking): $3.25
  Food, vitamins, miscellaneous: $94.45

Total: $326.05

I am glad I did not learn about economy from books but from the bedrock of experience. I discovered an America where I could practice the uncommon "game" of learning what it was like to "do without" and let my living be a "sport" rather than a "trade." Why was it fun? Because it was voluntary, yet it left my heart aching for those for whom it is a way of life filled with fear and insecurity.

Chapter 10
Gardening

Shall I not have intelligence with the earth? Am I not partly leaves and vegetable mould myself? What is the pill which will keep us well, serene, contented? Not my or thy great-grandfather's, but our great-grandmother Nature's universal, vegetable, botanic medicines, by which she has kept herself young always.

... Morning Air! If men will not drink at this fountainhead of the day, why, then we must bottle up some and sell it in the shops, for the benefit of those who have lost their subscription ticket to morning time in this world.[1]

Many will deny that I became a female Antaeus when I moved from my life of social involvement and clock-set rigidity to a life of comparative withdrawal, with the fewest obstacles to the rhythm of Nature's dictates of daylight and darkness. I chose my own portion of this earth's surface before the house was built. Without thinking, I took off my city-styled shoes and stood barefoot in the sand that surrounded my Walden III (for that is what I called it at first glance). Because I was invading the possession of a primitive and previous group of owners, the said owners, fire ants, bit me rather fiercely.

There being no apparent fertility in the land when I purchased it, it became my personal goal to make this desolate, desert-like

A WOMAN'S WALDEN

sand blossom as the rose. And where the fire ants went after the sod was laid can best be suspected by the stern admonition that older settlers pass on when they tell me not to walk barefoot in the dewy grass.

Though I have not planted seven miles of beans, I know what I have planted has special meaning for me. "My planting attached me to the earth so I got strength like Antaeus."[2] Why should I be so eager to plant? Has the tender nurturing of a tiny, struggling plant lengthened my maternal instincts past the child-bearing years? No. Have I not rather cast off those years and found in the labors of a female Antaeus a perpetual youth that reaches far beyond the external? Does the fact that every day's work is done partly in the earth itself contribute to the fact that I have rarely known loneliness, except in my travels when I have been cut off from the family of my own earth?

Again, are there perhaps two kinds of people on this earth? Those who live by Nature and those who live by trade? No. To those who know Nature only as a commodity by which to build an empire, seeking no other use, she remains man's mother and the place of his ultimate sleep. Yet even the tradesman leaves his high-rise apartment with its view of city skyscrapers for a vacation where other, pleasanter views may be seen.

I claimed heaven was my first purchase when I bought Walden III, though when I bought the land it was a stretch of unobstructed sky that stirred my heart. My pond became in that purchase a sea, for it holds the ocean of the sky in its moments of stillness. The mere vacationer cannot find the same pleasure in the view, or even in Nature itself, because for him it represents no more than a break in routine, a temporary kind of unreality before which he is the indulgent, uninvolved viewer.

Did my own involvement in nature grow from that early age in which I was sent to pick weeds out of the vegetable garden? If so, love grew out of hate, for I hated that interruption in my six-year-old's day. I had to be shown how similar were the leaves of a weed

Gardening

to that of the plant it sought to strangle and supplant. I was learning the life-long lesson of differentiation, to notice the subtle likenesses of infinitesimal contrasts between one plant and its enemy and, hence, between virtue and vice, between good and evil, between the tares and the wheat. I learned also that a plant must be very young if it is to survive the uprooting of a nearby weed; in that seemingly minor recognition, an understanding of space and time were added. In labor too often regarded as "primitive," we are granted an experience in more profound laws and moral powers than many of the so-called professions can grant. "What is a farm but a mute gospel? The chaff and the wheat, weeds and plants, blight, rain, insects, sun—it is a sacred emblem from the first furrow of spring to the last stack which the snow of winter overtakes in the fields."[3]

Although old settlers warn us against working when the dew is on, I would urge women especially to ignore any advice that admonishes us to "take it easy." "Do all your work if possible while the dew is on."[4] What is the "summer thought" which we must make our earth bring forth? We may be certain thoughts cannot be brought forth without labor. To believe they can be brought forth without effort is in effect to give over our earth to its natural crop of weeds. I will make it my daily work to show the affinity between gardening and my own thoughts while the dew is on the ground. "Labor of the hands" should be taught to every child early in his life. It should be given the honor it had in a pre-technological age. Unfortunately, it has been replaced with a byword, "Let George do it!" And George can be any*one* or any *machine*, whatever the situation demands.

"Labor of the hands, even when pursued to the verge of drudgery, is perhaps never the worst form of idleness. It has a constant and imperishable moral, and to the scholar it yields a classic result."[5] Of course, when I speak of "work of the hands" here, I refer to it in terms of gardening. To work directly in the earth itself is, for me, neither drudgery nor slave labor. It places

A WOMAN'S WALDEN

me in the location I like best, where the sky is my temple and the sun my candle. Here, my possibilities are so limitless it is always a surprise and an adventure to experience the relationship between the back-breaking labor of spading, harrowing (with a hand cultivator), planting, weeding, and watering, and one's thinking. I have often gone to my garden in moods of anger, resentment, frustration, discouragement, hopelessness, self-pity, or utter lassitude, and the miniature world of my plantings, a leaf, a drop of water clinging precariously to a blade of grass, a baby-fisted bud, a fiddle-head of fern has generated a sense of harmony that suggests an ultimate peace and ultimate triumph over my inner disharmonies.

Not that I have gone to the garden with any conscious thought that it should provide some sort of therapy. No, the urge has been virtually instinctive. I have gone out to my garden much as a child goes to its mother.

Often when other concerns have demanded my immediate energies and attention, I have perversely turned away from them in what the practical minded would call a waste of time. In fact, I am often asked, "How do you find time to work in the garden?" My unvarying answer is that I do it by neglecting something more pressing.

The answer does not originate with me but came from a critic. I have often been grateful for her intended rebuke, because it provides that Nature is not my secondary pursuit even though what she grants to me is a period of physical exertion that is idleness to my mind. The alternation of the body's activity in "work of the hands" with work of the mind yields the fruit of new and re-created thoughts.

One must not think from this that nature can be manipulated for ulterior purposes. One cannot leave the city with the secret design of wresting from nature the power to earn more money; she will not so divide her royalties. If we seek her merely for gain we shall find ourselves soundly mocked. Only need, that wordless

Gardening

searching of the child-mind, with its natural actions of necessity, will grant us that "other" dimension suggested by ancient poetry and mythology, "that husbandry was once a sacred art . . . ."[6]

By avarice, and selfishness, and a groveling habit, from which none of us is free, of regarding the soil as property, or the means of acquiring property chiefly, the landscape is deformed, husbandry is degraded with us and the farmer leads the meanest of lives. He knows Nature but as a robber.[7]

I think we should always, in every place our feet may touch, make that place of our sojourn more beautiful and more fruitful than we found it.

In keeping with this view, I have been a Mrs. Appleseed. An observer once asked curiously why I planted a garden in the spring when I had purposed to leave it for an extended absence. It struck them as wasteful, while I saw it as the loveliest of economies. It was my love letter to the earth for later tenants to enjoy and perhaps imitate. Again, such things are not taught; they are caught. Wherever I have lived I have planted trees, and I am now content in the knowledge that new owners are tending trees they bought but cannot own.

Accordingly, it was not surprising that my first gift to this piece of earth was the planting of three palm trees, three citrus trees, and three Italian cypress, with a silk oak, like a friendly sentinel, near my driveway. I had no idea when I selected a tree that would grace not merely the entrance to my house but the street as well, that an entirely subliminal reverence for the oak, as Grimm's fairy tales suggests it, may have been an active ingredient in my choice. The implication that the oak and the sky and the great god thunder are associated is one that any adult should consciously enjoy. As Frazer says, "A tree which had been struck by lightning is naturally regarded by the savage as

A WOMAN'S WALDEN

charged with a double or triple portion of fire; for has he not seen the mighty flash enter into the trunk with his own eyes?"[8] Why should our sophistication rob us of the recognition that, in spite of technology, a power does, indeed, descend from the skies? Of course, we explain it away by citing the fact that electricity passes more easily through oak than any other tree. Superstitious or not, I will continue to regard its branches as a "visible emanation" of God's power.

Other trees have subsequently been added, but these are my basic ten. Would that tree planting could become an added feature of our yearly Thanksgiving rites which seem nowadays to have degenerated into a festival of food signifying little more than that our national god is our stomach.

In this regard I do not simply preach; I practice. The return of a son who escaped death in the war prompted my personal "Magnificat." In gratitude for his life and safe return, I planted a blue spruce that will always be our "Loren Tree."

Is there something of symbolic futurism in my present preoccupation with the cultivation of soil on the banks of my Walden III? Did my earliest play making mud-pies have any bearing on what I do today? True, the contents of those early concoctions have nothing to do with the real pies I now make; it may well be that a mysterious internal process was set in motion whereby one makes a later return to those "first-fruits" granted to us when we were children. We know that nearly all societies of men saw the sacrament of presenting "first-fruits" in many different forms, and this, together with the theory of *transference*, does not make the relationship of mud-pies to my present love for horticulture too farfetched.

Not farfetched at all is the warfare of weeds as it parallels the uprooting of faults. When, instead of carrying the weeds to the compost pile, I let them lie under the shade of some cultivated leaf, thus sheltered from the sun, raise themselves upright again. When we relate this to our human faults, which we keep in the

Gardening

shade of some virtue where the sun of truth cannot reach its roots, we see that there it grows to be very like that root of bitterness whereby many are defiled. For the uprooting of faults, only "a continual motion, repastination, and turning of the mold"[9] will do.

There are so many ways to break up the fallow ground of truth, but when we alternate one crop with the main crop in order to nourish the soil, many regard it as a waste. In viewing the human field, truth cannot produce the harvest it might unless it is first planted with a green manure (experiences that must be turned over and buried by either a plow or a spade). How convincingly Nature's succession of plants shows us that human beings have the same needs.

Not merely for the sake of a harvest should every crop seek to escape frost. In this I will be equally concerned about the frosts of indifference and neglect in the cultivation of sincerity, truth, simplicity, faith, innocence, and the like. In the vacancies of my own life I will be careful to plant new crops, and where even these crops are worm-eaten, I will look to the soil. Surely our natures have their natural growth and will produce either weeds or wheat. I will be careful to water the grain and destroy the weeds.

In all this my greatest labor grows from an easiness I did not easily reach. Because it is so regular and impartial to all, I take for granted that all growth in my garden comes not from me but that "principle cultivator"[10] the sun, which rises on the just and unjust alike. In my mind I must learn to set aside all concern for results and take no credit for whatever the harvest may be. If the first-fruits of my life brought me unthinkingly back to Nature, so that mud-pies and weeding had their uses without effort on my part, then this should grant me that easiness which eases all anxiety in daily work. My life's *last fruits* should enable me to see that "every end is converted into a new means."[11]

Chapter 11
Neighbors

If a man does not keep pace with his companions,
perhaps it is because he hears a different drummer.
Let him step to the music that he hears,
however measured or far away.
It is not important that he should mature
as soon as an apple tree or an oak.
Shall he turn his spring into summer?
If the condition of things which we are made for
is not yet, what were any reality which we can substitute?
We will not be shipwrecked on a vain reality.[1]

In a certain sense I did not need to leave my home to find Walden. My objection to remaining where I was lay in the fact that I was **living** a series of roles that earning a living demanded. In order to transact my own private business, it was necessary to be free of the need to earn money, to live one year of my life as deliberately as the earth itself. The movement of the sun would be the only "clock" I would obey. Conformity to the demands of multiplied particulars would no longer be permitted to scatter my force.

The fact that I have neighbors has, if anything, contributed to my solitude. Any projected image of me must be permitted to rest in the eyes of the beholder. For the most part, those who claim to know me are engaged, as Emerson has said, in a game of blind

A WOMAN'S WALDEN

man's buff. One who judges me from the viewpoint of his own reality has touched on no more than one small particular of my total person. I will not attach my own self-view to it. To do so would be to conform to another's image of me. The end result would make me subservient to an opinion. Who knows how many opinions I might be led to serve, or how false I might become in trying to live up to several versions of projected images? At best, another's view can be no more than half-truth and to conform to such would place anyone in a prison house of conformity.

It is clear that my solitude exists apart from all sense of place or proximity of people. And no romanticist will persuade me that marriage compounded of love invades that solitude. It is rather as Rilke describes it: "Love consists in this, that two solitudes protect and touch and greet each other."

Perhaps no kindlier view of human personality can be found than in the vegetable kingdom. There it is not resemblances or similarities that are valued but variety. Among people we seem to fear differences. Why? As Cato said, "Difference begets contradiction; contradiction begets heat; heat rises into resentment, rage, ill-will. Thus they differ in affection, as they differ in judgment, and the contention which began in pride, ends in anger."

Why are the differences in plants, both cultivated and parasitic, given more acceptance and toleration than human differences? Why should we exercise more care in selecting the soil for an onion or a petunia than we do in selecting the "soil" of our own lives? We accept and propagate differences between plants, while we strive to perpetuate conformity on the human level.

Jane is totally dependable as well as adaptable. It matters little whether her life's day is sunny or partially shaded; Jane adjusts. True, she does not aspire to outdo her neighbors. Perhaps this is why she is of the long-flowering sort. In her flower parallel, she is known as *Ageratum housatonianum*.

Neighbors

Alice requires purified soils. If not, she is subject to attacks of illness. Also, she needs support to which she should be attached. If she is to produce her best bloom, she must have many a would-be flower cut away. "Pinched" at six inches is the recommended procedure, in order that larger and longer stemmed flowers may develop. Her floral name is snapdragon.

Grace can tolerate intense heat, and grows in every color except blue. She can claim three different careers. Next to a house or building, she is used for bedding and borders. Inside the house her brilliant colors appear as zinnias.

Hope is credited with extra-sensory powers. Though she grasps at impossibilities in her innocent, unsuspecting serenity, she makes any life an easier journey. Seventeenth-century herbalists gave her a series of saints' names, of which only three survive: St. John's, St. Peter's and St. Andrew's Wort (wort meaning herbaceous plant). She is credited with curing eye diseases, skin irritations, gall stones and melancholia. Hope remains an all-purpose remedy.

Contrary to legend, Joyce thrives on neglect. Prolific and rapid growing, her children grow from a long graceful cascade of shiny green which makes her blossoms resemble small birds on a branch. Joyce is the *Cymbidium orchid*.

Lynn is dramatic and spectacular, a dancer in a flaring skirt of red with white "petticoat" petals. Her sister is dressed in a bell-shaped crinoline with an upward curving rose colored skirt. Of course both of them are *fuchsias*.

Carol has yellow eyes, and I am tempted to ask her if she is wearing contact lenses. She is dressed in a ruffled, bell-shaped skirt, and cannot endure the touch of water or storms. If you will give her a sheltered environment when she is fully mature, she will cover her entire body in fluffy blossoms which we call *begonias*.

Jean is a jewel. Though often moody, she is everyone's favorite, and for all her moods and susceptibilities, she remains the world's

A WOMAN'S WALDEN

first choice. Christ himself shares her name as we sing each Christmas, "Lo, how a rose e'er blooming."

Jack is every boys' first hero, and dates from prehistoric times. Because he is quick and vigorous, and very dramatic, it is easy to see why he became a legend. Indeed, evidence of his offspring have been found in Peru, Brazil, Canada, New England, and the Carolinas. Originally he came from Phaselis, a town in Pamphylia. He is very impatient, the result, no doubt of his speedy vigor, which also accounts for his wide-spread travel. If one omits the "and" he is Jack the beanstalk, familiarly known as lima, bush or pole bean.

Many years had to pass before Joe's worth became known. His greatest contribution can only be achieved if he is granted regular rest periods. Yet he cannot rest unless the weather is forbidding. This has kept him out of the tropics. It is also true that he finds it impossible to develop his talents unless he is given much space, or a large margin of error. When these requirements are met, one can follow Cato's directions laid down two thousand years ago, when Pliny claimed that asparagus grew to be as heavy as three pounds.

Bill was, in ancient times, presented to Apollo, being born on the coast of the Mediterranean, as far east as the Caspian Sea and Persia. He has four children, and it is not difficult to understand why the Greeks made use of him in paying homage to Apollo. "His name comes from the fact that when the seed pods swell they look like the Greek letter 'beta' B." Botanists identify his offspring as Swiss chard or leaf beet, sugar beet, stock beet and the ordinary *garden beet*.

Carl has been written about in records found in China in 1300, Japan in 1712, India in 1826, Arabia in 1775, European herbalists in 1536, Virginia in 1609, Brazil in 1647. He is not at all picky about his location, and can tolerate a wide variety of temperatures. His popularity in America can be seen from his commercial increase. Acreage devoted to *carrots* increased from

Neighbors

9,770 acres in 1923 to 43,500 in 1939.

Walter originally came from the Incas in South America, from whence he was brought to Spain. Probably someone in Spain brought him to America, but this is not certain. In 1585 his brown skin was an intense disappointment to his owner in Ireland. He was condemned as "poisonous and mischievous" and accused of causing leprosy and dysentery. In 1619, King James I allowed him in his household because he had a reputation for being "exotic." By the year 1846 he had become so influential that this "rich man's luxury became the poor man's bread." Yes, the *potato* changed the very history of Ireland.

George traces his origin back to the Garden of Eden, and Pliny tells us he was a sort of Roman medicine man. He "could cure the sting of serpents, heal watery eyes, and give utterance to those rendered suddenly speechless. Egyptians said he resembled the universe, since in their cosmogeny the various spheres of heaven, earth, and hell were concentric." What would cooks do without the *onion!*

Chapter 12
Retirement Village, U.S.A.

It is remarkable how easily and insensibly we fall into a particular route, and make a beaten track for ourselves . . . . How worn and dusty, then, must be the highways of the world, how deep the ruts of tradition and conformity.[1]

Where is Retirement Village, U.S.A., located? East or west, north or south, the choice is yours. However, my neighbor cannot speak English, though we both live in a town known for its "Cadillacs and cardiacs." She drives her Cadillac into her garage, and parks it on a worn-out oriental carpet brought down from a house "up north." From her broken English I learn that the up-north-home was in the Polish section of New York City, not far from Stuyvesant Town. Her retirement home has a new wall-to-wall carpet, and all new furniture of which her husband says, "It iss yoost like vee vass nooly-veds!" Their house is immaculate. Portraits from Europe adorn the walls; stern faces peer out of their convex glass and dark backgrounds at the yellow, lime and and orange gaiety of a senior citizen's "golden age" decorating choices.

When I say I am a misfit with my three-speed Vega (1973), and my antiques from Brooklyn, I say it more in sorrow than in superiority. I weep for all of us. Another neighbor who has lived here five years says matter-of-factly, though the bitterness and

A WOMAN'S WALDEN

disappointment cannot be concealed from her voice, "No, my children have not seen our retirement home, but I remind myself," she adds mournfully, "that they have their own lives to live. We educated them, and what did we get for it? Nothing!" Nonetheless, she is the envy of every price-conscious neighbor. I wonder how much of her artsy-craftsy home has been purchased to fill an emptiness that her fourteen-hundred-dollar drapes and her costly knick-knacks could never fill?

What of the men? When they aren't shopping for a new model car, a boat, or even a motorcycle, they are golfing from motorized carts while their stomachs protrude perilously forward. Both their stance and that little white ball are in competition with those pie-pregnancies. Also, they meet once a week to practice their Sweet Adeline barbershop songs. Forget about the quartets and quintets of their youth, that would eliminate too many men who want to sing along. Besides, a big group helps to reduce inhibitions. you can hear their loud guffaws, and their D.O.M. jokes, if you care to listen at the door of the clubhouse. Since I have my information from a woman who did just that, she assures me the humor differed in no particular from the current teen-age, locker-room variety.

A youthful visitor, upon hearing "D.O.M." with reference to a distinguished-looking white-haired man, asked if the term was a contraction for the ministerial "Dominie." Her informant, a petite little lady of eighty-three, laughed delightedly and said, "My dear, I hate to disillusion you, but it stands for dirty old man, and he can't keep his hands off me!" At the look of shock on the face of her eighteen-year-old visitor, she added acidly, "Don't be so naive! He has probably taken you to bed in his fantasies more than once! Not that he would or could, you understand." Of course these remarks caused the generation gap to become whole continents wider. It is not at all what the average eighteen-year-old girl suspects of old age. How could she suspect? The frank

Retirement Village, U.S.A.

little eighty-three year old school teacher of the above account is a rare example of old age.

The neatness of the green lawns and the variations in landscape architecture are a source of endless fascination to the sunrise walker, of which I appear to be the only woman. I *do* see several women in varying styles of nightgowns and robes walk out to their driveways for the morning papers at that hour. I wonder if they take note of the editorial which states that they are living among 631,358 adults classified as illiterate? I also meet men who are walking, jogging or bicycling. It would be out of order for me to ask, "Do you miss the Long Island Railroad? The subway? The commuter trains from New Jersey? Do you miss your deadline-oriented life at the office?"

Appearance bears little or no relationship to reality in old age, or any age, for that matter, and like that white-haired "Dominie" there are some interesting reversals. I learn that some of the most elegantly dressed retirement men were plumbers, brick-layers and construction workers, whereas a college professer who once flunked a student for "improper dress" finds his compensatory old-age costume in dressing as shabbily as he once dressed conservatively. To each his own. It probably would please him to know that his neighbors refer to him as a "displaced hippy."

Did I mention that landscape planting choices are perhaps more revealing than fashions and faces? I pass a lawn that resembles the Morse Code. What subliminal SOS has this man planted with his dot-dot-dash of cement-circled bushes?

Farther along is the home of an artist. All of the characters from Snow White and the Seven Dwarfs are frolicking colorfully, if woodenly, among the trees. Tsk, tsk, Mr. Disney, such an influence you have had!

Next is a lawn, if you can call it that, which informs me of my need for smoked glasses. Stark white pebbles extend from white sidewalk to white house. There is one tree squarely planted in the center with not even a ring of black soil to assist its struggle

A WOMAN'S WALDEN

for life. My eyes rest with relief on the greenness of the lawn next door. Its plantings would earn it an "A" for horticultural patchwork quilting, so many and so various are its greens. The next lawn specializes in a dry version of the Thousand Islands. Flower beds, or "islands" as they are called here, form an obstacle course for any lawn-mower or lawn-care service. I learn, via gossip, that these people hate sunlight and their neighbors, and I am almost convinced that this is true. I wonder how the mailman finds his way to the mail slot in the front door. And what have they got against fresh air? Their high stockade fence effectively eliminates any stray breeze that might decide to be friendly.

Questions are raised in my mind as I approach one of the most elegantly planted lawns in our area. This couple made no secret of being late-blooming lovers; they re-married after years of bereaved loneliness. Their house is appropriately framed in greenery and has an unbroken expanse of lawn that makes their property seem larger than that of their over-planted neighbors. To the rear is a luxurious free-form swimming pool. It is reported that the interior of the house was decorated by a prestigious member of the local A.I.D. Why does an equally outstanding firm have a sign here which reads, "For Sale"? Did these lovers find that the dreams they wrapped in expenditures wore no armor for reality? Their divorce is pending.

Finally, I arrive at my favorite corner. Though this little portion of Retirement Village, U.S.A. is five years old, the size of the trees belie the fact. They seem to have guarded this corner for a generation at least. I pause to speak to the owner, who is a sunrise collector like myself, a man who looks like a member of the Mafia until he takes you on his tree tour. Then he turns abruptly to say, "Sh-sh-sh, they're having babies!" as he points to his "village" of bird houses, and you learn that you have met a member of an unusual, as yet unnamed, human society. I call him the president of The Humane Heart Society, for his sensitivity to the needs of others extends far beyond birds and trees. He also

Retirement Village, U.S.A.

cares for those much harder to care for: human beings. He would be embarrassed if he knew about the data I have collected on his unobtrusive, unassuming helpfulness to a wide variety of ethnically diverse people.

Why do I weep for *all* of these senior citizen Utopias? Wherever you have senior citizen housing, whether rented or owned, you have segregation in one of its most virulent forms. With our lives we have signed the papers which say (if not actually at least by inference), "We must segregate ourselves from our children. We know we are not wanted. They must be free to live their own lives. We must find locations which will give us maximum creature comforts for an interim existence between the end of our parenting days and our nursing-home futures."

Interview such people, and you will find they feel "closer" to Hudson, Rose, or Lord Bellamy's son of T.V.'s *Upstairs, Downstairs* than they do to their adult children.

Bicycle after sunset as I do, and see in every darkened window that one huge light is on. What is it? The T.V. It is the perfect anesthetic for loneliness. The psycho-surgical separation of the thirty-nine-year-old parental umbilical cord is effectively accomplished with that "plug-in drug." Those self-extensions, our children, and our childrens' children—have we no place in their lives? Resignation, or what Thoreau termed "confirmed desperation" is the *fait accompli*. No, not for everyone. A private survey has informed me of some who have moved back and forth as many as five times. What wealth, or what scrounging have many of our restless seniors accumulated or practiced? My neighbor, whose Cadillac idles on the oriental rug, had his machine shop, and his wife was a restaurant cook. What deferred living are they making up for?

Aging women take refuge in real or imagined illnesses, but, whatever its causes, the pain is *always* real. For a price, they buy their comforts from a series of doctors whose fees mount yearly, as the traffic will bear. There are doctors, whose contempt for

A WOMAN'S WALDEN

idleness is revealed in callous office practices and personnel who keep the aged waiting three and four hours in their magazine-stacked waiting rooms for their appointments. Grinning, these over-worked doctors reply to their colleagues, "Well, (Hell?) what else do they have but time?"

To digress, notice the "new" medical office décor. In a sampling of ten doctors from the east coast to the west coast, I noted the absence of the cozy engulfing easy chair and the occasional rocker. These have been replaced with straight-backed, plastic covered chairs which take less room, deferring, no doubt, to increased numbers of patients and our multi-millions of backaches.

One wonders why the increase in qualified doctors never seems to match a similar disproportionate increase in people seeking help. It requires no subtlety of mind to understand that medical groups must protect their exclusivity at the expense of their services to suffering fellow humans, especially when their underwriters are Medicare and Medicaid, along with millions of oldsters too mentally tired to deal *ad infinitum* with long, confusing forms.

I have become a self-appointed objector. Yes, I must agree to let my children live their own lives. I did. But not once in a long lifetime of living my own life have I had to exclude or ignore those who gave me life. In youthful selfishness I admit I was motivated by self-interest. That ancient decree, "Honour thy father and thy mother *that it may be well with thee*," [2] figured prominently in my good deeds. It was bargain-basement morality of the lowest kind, with overtones of fear and superstition. But so effective are such ancient and tested words that when I had perfunctorily shared my youth-centered, selfish life with my (we-have-nothing-in-common!) parents, my personal rewards were rich beyond all I could ask or think. When I became a parent myself, and passed out of that you-don't-understand-me stage, my legalistic "honor" changed. A common basis, parenthood, bypassed self-interest,

Retirement Village, U.S.A.

and we entered into that level of love which truly cares for the well-being of another.

Moreover, at Christmas, when I saw my blind and deaf eighty-three-year-old mother with *my* three-year-old grandchild, (*her* great-grandchild), I took careful notes. It was a family gathering at which all the beautiful and young mothers of my grandchildren were present. Yet over and over the little ones—the preschool, wee ones—gravitated instinctively to my frail and wrinkled mother. Spontaneously, they singled out great-grandma as *their* special person. They kissed her, they stroked her, and hoisted themselves onto her lap (she weighs only ninety-eight pounds). At least two of them said, as they tentatively ran small fingers over her cheeks, "You're old, aren't you?" Then she sang children's songs from her own youth in Europe, in a language they did not understand. At one point she got up, and in her crackling voice, she sang and did a tottery little dance to show them what they did in Norway. Clapping her hands as she sang "Da tenner moder alle lys, og ingenkrok er mork!" ("Then mother lights our candles, and not a corner is dark!") Those of us past forty felt the momentary sting of tears at seeing our own soon-coming frailties personified.

But what did the children see? They were filled with delight at seeing, quite subconsciously, their own inadequacies and imperfections in a grown-up! How tender they were to her after that performance, as if to say, "We're not so great either, but now we won't be afraid to *be* not great!"

The absolute joy on great-grandma's face was also a glimpse of how important the mixing of the generations can be. We *all* need each other! Who knows what future solidarity a unified family can provide? If anyone lives beyond the three-score-years-and-ten, their strength may indeed be "sorrow and heaviness," but their very presence teaches us endurance, teaches us the tenacity and value of life *just as it is.*

If social change is to take place, it must begin with those who

A WOMAN'S WALDEN

have the time and leisure to change it. The social-security group represents an untapped reservoir of potential social service. In the interim period between active parental responsibility and a nursing-home future, retirees should *use* their leisure. As volunteer grandparents they could give neglected little children some "hands-on" loving and rocking. They could give such little ones a "we-were-there" sense of history, and foster a strength for coping with changes these children must inevitably face. Grandparents, through the proof of age, can be the means of making *change* a little less fearful, passing on that most priceless of all intangibles, hope. Above all, we must guard against passing on our losses and our defeats! Love and laughs and hope and old-fashioned values which say a drop of cold water given in love will never lose its reward—these are the things we must dedicate ourselves to pass on.

Labor for retirees? At the other end of the population spectrum are the nursing homes. We *must*, and we *can*, see that our own parents do not die alone and among strangers! "But you don't know how crazy my old lady can be!" some may say. It does not take a nurse's training to teach us *not to react*. Average intelligence should make us see our aged as, in some cases, twice-children, with none of the adorable physical attractiveness of children. This makes them twice as needy! Retirees should repeat Amy Carmichael's words every day of their lives: "From silken self, deliver me!"

Are we worried about the youth of today? We must stop *telling* them to change, and show them *our* change! It does no good to rationalize, "I've worked hard all my life; I owe it to myself to get some fun out of life." At any age, the fun-syndrome is self-defeating if it is not related to effort and struggle that reaches beyond such self-preserving efforts as jogging or other pursuits that circulate around the self.

That is not to say I am against fun. An ancient line proclaims, "Laughter is health to the bones;" I can find a laugh every day of

Retirement Village, U.S.A.

my life within the confines of a job, because I make it my business to look for laughter, or provide it for another. But to pursue fun for its own sake is to require ever greater stimuli for the surfeiting that such a search inevitably brings.

So brace yourselves, my children! I'm coming back from this geriatric ghetto.

As an adult I mean to give you a "hands-off" love.

"Ha!" you say. "Intentions!"

No, they are more than that. I have prepared for this stage of life by earning two college degrees in "old age" (after forty), and I shall never cease to wrestle with disciplined study. "My mind to me a kingdom is," is more than verse, and I know the pitfalls of psychosomatic ailments. My adult offspring *shall* remember me as humorous, idea-centered, busy and involved, rather than a collector of real or imagined slights. I don't care what learned label of psychological dependency is tacked upon me. I shall not, and I cannot, amputate or segregate my mothering years.

This does not mean that I expect my children to move in the orbit of my life as they did in childhood. I want no more than to be a satellite in their lives, to stand on the outskirts of their comings and goings. I want them to come (yes, even dutifully), to my fussy, family dinners, because I refuse to be part of those bold-faced lies I hear on every side. "We don't belong in their lives anymore!" I do. I cannot un-mother my heart.

Chapter 13
Former Inhabitants

Be but thy inspiration given,
  No matter through what danger sought,
I'll fathom hell or climb to heaven,
  And yet esteem that cheap which love has bought.[1]

The snowstorms of 1977 reminded me of winters I have weathered in the past. Treacherous ice concealed by snow once caught me off guard, and in protecting my derriere with outspread palms, I broke my right arm. After surgery the break became an authentic rationale for permanently impaired penmanship.

I think of a winter in the fifth grade when it was my task to hold the reins for a team of horses on the North Dakota prairie. I was the eldest of a group of six children whose only means of transport to and from the prairie school was a grain wagon sled. While I held the reins, it could hardly be said that I was the driver. The horses, Dexter and Prince, found their own way as the five children huddled down in the hay under fur rugs, with feet against bricks hot from the kitchen oven. I held the slack reins, unable to see so much as the ears of the horses through the opaque layers of snowflakes. We were in an unmarked ocean of a swirling white blizzard. The only sound was the even, plodding crunch of the horses' hooves in the powdery snow. Two and a half miles later, as we drew near the still-invisible farm house, we savored

A WOMAN'S WALDEN

the prospect of our safe arrival. The woofs of Barry, our dog, led us home.

School children in such circumstances equate home with a paradise of warmth. From a black-lidded kitchen stove, the odor of newly-baked bread emerges, and an oasis of light hallows the old round table as a peacefully murmured m-m-m-m sounds from the big teakettle at the back of the stove.

There was no sterile neatness in such kitchens. Our snow-wet mittens were draped on the doors of the two warming ovens, one at each side of the chimney. Coats were hung on the clothes tree in the corner. Then, before we could have our after-school snack of warm bread and runny jam or brown sugar, we were pointed toward the small black cistern pump to wash our hands in the gray agate basin at the wash stand.

If we were still hungry, one of us would lift up the cellar lid by its big brass ring recessed into the flooring. A step ladder led down to an earthen darkness where the smell of loam mingled with a spicy apple smell. Rude shelves, three deep with mason jars, lined the dirt walls. A sweet-grass basket full of apples in one hand left the other hand free to maneuver the climb back up the ladder, and the lid to the cellar was quickly dropped to keep the precious kitchen warmth from escaping. But materialism has destroyed the poetry of homecoming. We have all become "key children" and the door to home is the door to a place to sleep, a rootless, "anywhere that I can make a dollar."

If nostalgia and a glorification of the past were my only motives, it would have been easier to rent a place with the very inconveniences I have described. However, I believe my motives were nearer to Zilpha's though I have changed the words she murmured over her gurgling pot. Instead of, "Ye are all bones, bones!" I ask myself, "Can these bones live?" The self-appointed scribe of a latter-day Walden, I must rattle the bones and see what happens.

After any conflict, it is a common custom to relate the bravery

Former Inhabitants

or cowardice that events bring forth, for if life shares only its wealth and favor with us we would never choose retirement and solitude. We require the prodding of some pain which drives us into a corner, and in the idleness of that corner—sometimes called "the Red Sea place," or "the winter of our discontent"—we rise to newness of life.

What were the former inhabitants of Florida like? Where more than 45,000 now live there were only twenty families in 1924. When the freight and passenger train arrived each Friday all the people in town would go to meet it, though often there would be no more than one or two passengers.

News of this city was reported in a Brooklyn newspaper in 1903; perhaps the power of the pen is nowhere more life-changing than in the advent of what became known as "The America Letter." A transplanted Scandinavian living in Brooklyn decided to send a city newspaper to a friend in Finland because his friend Ole was a seaman who could read English. Ole's wife saved the precious mail until her husband came home from a trip to Africa. During his stay at home, Ole chafed under the frigid winter weather. House-bound, he found himself reading a glowing account of how one could buy land in Florida. Fast-growing oranges, lemons and grapefruit with vegetables between the tree rows would nourish the soil and produce a saleable crop for a hungry world. Imagine the sunshine of a tropical climate. Ole's wife was expecting her first child; the great appeal for her was having her husband home twenty-four hours a day. Selling their little home in Finland, they boarded an ocean liner for Ellis Island. In New York harbor they boarded another boat for Jacksonville, Florida.[2]

Traveling from Jacksonville to Tampa by train they learned that they would have to travel by mule and wagon to the land company they had read about in the Brooklyn newspaper in Finland. When they arrived, Ole's wife asked where the city was and learned there were only twelve families, living in what

A WOMAN'S WALDEN

appeared to be a jungle. Their disappointment was tempered somewhat by their purchase of twenty acres of land.

Another resident (I'll call him George), lives a mile from my pond, and his father learned about Florida from a traveling salesman who boarded the railroad where he worked. Sight unseen, he purchased forty acres of land.

Jim, a Massachusetts school teacher, came to this area for his health, and in 1926 saw that an elementary school was constructed. Not far from the school is the courthouse where misdemeanors of the past received an early version of what is now known as plea-bargaining. The judge would hand the prisoner a Sears Roebuck catalogue and tell him to open it and put his finger on the first item on the page. "Whatever the cost of the article would be the amount of the fine imposed whether it was a ten-cent strainer or an eight ninety-five suit. One man who ended up in the judge's court remarked, 'I'm sure glad they don't sell big boats or cars in that catalogue.' "[3]

However, in considering former inhabitants, any year after 1900 gives us a former inhabitant of relatively modern dimension. This earth I walk on gives now no hint of what a thousand men had once hoped to find here. DeSoto's men came to Florida in response to rumors that the conqueror of Peru, having brought huge quantities of silver, gold and precious stones, was investing his fortune in a second venture. Men of distinguished rank, as well as civilians and laborers, with youth as their main qualification, organized in little more than a year an armada of seven ships.

The armada was equipped with enormous supplies of "crude iron, steel, iron for saddle bows, spades, pick axes, crates, ropes and baskets, all of which were necessary for colonization,"[4] with double rations of every kind of ship supply. After their arrival in Florida they endured incredible hardships, of which the battle of Mauvila in 1540 was the worst. Out of a force of "six or seven thousand warriors," DeSoto's men killed all but one Indian who,

Former Inhabitants

circling his neck with a noose, leaped from the wall of the fort and killed himself. It was a victory that left them with all supplies, all food, all shelter, all clothing destroyed by a fire they themselves had set in the midst of the battle.[5] By actual count they found that there were "a thousand seven hundred and seventy-odd treatable wounds, . . . for scarcely a man among them was not injured, and most of them have five and six wounds, whereas many had ten and twelve."[6] With no medicines, no bandages, no pain killers (their liquor had been burned), no huts, no clothing with which to cover themselves from the night air, and in many cases, unable to so much as stand because of loss of blood, how could they survive?

Like soldiers, or troubled people everywhere, they groaned their pain-wracked foxhole prayers, and were aided by ideas unthinkable apart from the indomitable will to survive. Rallying their forces, the least wounded aided those who had received the most serious injuries. Bowers of branches made hovels against the few remaining walls of the great Indian fort. By opening the bodies of dead Indians, fat and oils were found for the treatment of wounds. Shirts and other clothing from dead Spaniards became dressings. Dead horses were skinned for meat, and straw was gathered for pallets. "During this time thirteen Spaniards died because of their inability to obtain medical attention. (There was one doctor.) Forty-seven had perished in the battle, eighteen of whom had been killed by arrows shot through their eyes or mouth, for the Indians, on perceiving that their bodies were protected by armour, aimed at their faces. In addition to those Christians who died during the battle, and afterward before they could receive treatment, another twenty-two succumbed because of inadequate supply of medicine and doctors. Therefore we may say that in all eighty-two Spaniards were lost in the battle of Mauvila."[7]

When at length a band of less than three hundred men, haggard, barefooted, and clothed in animal skins were welcomed to Mexico City by Viceroy Don Antonio de Mendoza, their experiences brought them no internal peace. Dissension between them reached such a pitch that "they fell to slashing one another with rabidness and a desire to kill."[8] Their fury with one another grew as they compared the cultivated fields of Mexico with the forty provinces of fertile abundance they had left in Florida. "Finally, they remembered the great wealth of pearls and seed pearls they had scorned, and the splendors in which they had seen themselves, for each man had fancied himself as the Lord of a great province. And as they compared those riches and noble estates with their present miseries and paucities, some discussed their visions and melancholy thoughts with others, and with most sorrowful hearts and self-pity remarked:.... 'Were not the lands we left better than these where at present we are?' "[9] They had come full circle back to their first discontent.

In their youth in Spain it had been to a *future* wealth they had looked forward. In their return they looked to the past. When every consolation was offered them, they were tormented by regret for having scorned and abandoned what they had once possessed.

Where was the new life to be found? Many of these same men returned to Spain to enter religious orders, "so as to dignify all their past life with a fine end."[10] Yet by their return to Spain, does not the record of their lives tell us that the new is always found in the old?

Chapter 14
The Pond

Heaven is under our feet as well as over our heads.[1]

My view of any pond in proportion to the earth's size is to subjectively relate it to the pupil of my eye, in ratio to the size of my body. I know I am enamored by the fact that such a speck on this planet is able to contain in its placid little surface the immensity of heaven itself. Yes, it is "earth's eye."

The pond is such a humble patch of liquid devoid entirely of the threatening roar and mystery of the ocean. Here there is no wild rush of water, no dark brooding whirls of violence such as I have experienced in sea voyages. Here there is no restless, wind-filled vehemence, and no water-creatures common to the sea; no tritons, no mermaids, no sirens, no menacing shapes. Nothing shatters this calm, protected sense of an agreeable loneliness. All is gentle and benevolent; nothing mars this quiet stretch of water and sky.

Is this to say that all is tame and intimately domestic? No. For me, it unites the landscape with sky and clouds. Without the sky, its source of opalescent fire, the pond would be merely the scene of shadowy homes, and a dark mirror for the trees that grow around it. As it lies in one of earth's dimples, it transforms the image of passing clouds into undulating shapes much like the quivering reflections one sees in a Monet or Cezanne painting, in which the clear image is broken down to allow the imagination the freedom

A WOMAN'S WALDEN

to grasp something elusively beyond the merely external.

At times I wonder if our gravitation to ponds is a subconscious search for synthesis. Is it an attempt to find another and deeper reality beyond what is momentary and fleeting? Since it is, in fact, "Sky-Water," does it unite both the rational and irrational aspects of our nature in symbolic parallel?

Thoreau writes, "It is a mirror which no stone can crack. Whose quick-silver will never wear off, whose gilding Nature continually repairs; no storms, no dust, can dim its surface ever fresh;—a mirror in which all impurity presented to it sinks, swept and dusted by the sun's hazy brush—this light dust cloth—which retains no breath that is breathed on it, but sends its own to float as clouds high above its surface, and be reflected in its surface still."[2]

But we are never satisfied with merely seeing. We are continually bringing our understanding and our intellect to bear on all that we look at. This is why we need the repetition of "precept upon precept; line upon line"[3] to look and look and look again. Otherwise we will see only what the eye registers. This is also why I will not look at the lake of glass commonly referred to as television. The rapidity of visual imagery seems significantly designed to exclude my mind. A mesmerizing mental paralysis renders all my responses shallow and treats my brain as if it were no more than a mechanical recording device.

Just now I am "wasting" time in silent conversation with the pond. But who can say whether my so-called inactivity is not an ordered activity of a higher sort? True communication is not always found in reasoning and analysis. How much genuine communication takes place in listening? What am I listening for? I do not know. But I know that my own voice must be silent, because I want to be far away from that "dead echo" which is self calling unto myself, and the time I lose in silence will be harvested in a wider activity than mere busy-ness could grant me. It will be said, "Aha! You are not simply wasting time. There

The Pond

is method in your madness." But the idea of a wider harvest did not come until the wasted silence had let its silence be heard. It will, in its sequel, have a thousand interpretations in as many minds.

Sitting in silence at the water's edge, I did learn that my pursuits must be *peculiar* to myself, and its effect in any wider harvest will be measured by its effect in my own life. Again, it must be said the results in my own life will defy definition, which brings us up against the final mystery that resides in silence. Our world demands accounting, and idle meditation on a pond cannot be made to fit into columns of debits and credits.

Just now my eye registers the fact that the pond is dark grey and ruffled, and the fact that it is shadowed in drab colors dramatizes the absence of the sun. I must be content in recognizing that the pond is not now alive with the sun and the sky, but with the animation born of wind. At certain times wind and sun unite and the feathery waves are no longer dappled shades of grey, but turn into sparkling crescents too bright for the eye to look at steadily. I am peculiarly glad that it receives its color from the sky and the sun, and its animation from the wind. If I could look directly down at its surface would I note that "a still subtler spirit sweeps over it?"[2]

I am not a fisher-woman, but I have a genuine admiration for men who can sit for hours waiting for a nibble on their lines, or those who wade in and catch a mess of fish in a hurry. I am often asked how the fish got into our pond. I have no knowledge of it being stocked with fish, but I see men across the pond catching them, and I remember being told how fish spawn is carried by cranes and wading birds from one pond to another. Such birds easily carry a few eggs on their beak, as they are known to mash their catch before swallowing the wriggling fish. We don't know for sure how it is done, but we know remote lakes and ponds that have neither inlet nor outlet have fish in them.

The wealth and variety of subtle color in fish speaks to me of an

A WOMAN'S WALDEN

infinite love of beauty and diversity. I love to sit quietly at the water's edge and watch their water-ballet when I throw crumbs on the surface. There is the upward arch, then the delicate inhaling of the morsel, with an almost simultaneous half-circle down-swing.

All the while the fish are cavorting there is an aerial ballet above me. An airy pinwheel flings his gray slender body with white wing patches through the air trailing musical notes in an invisible cascade of carols. He is the Florida mockingbird. Meanwhile, a motionless white head with a yellow beak stands in the green water grasses of my shore patiently waiting for a passing fish. The egret *casmerodius albus* is a permanent resident of my pond, with his snowy white plume among the tufts of tall water weeds. Perhaps the most persistent solo intrument in my symphony and ballet of birds is the treble fall of the three protracted and melancholy "loo, loo, loo" of the coral footed mourning dove. He blends well with the bass fiddle of the mallard ducks, and the creaking complaints of the ever-present gulls as they circle overhead, as if theirs were a far nobler flash of flight than the scavenging trips we know they are taking. For me, they are the aerial parallel to the sea-mists not far away.

The perfect grace notes in my bird-ballet are the sandpipers. A migrant bird in Florida, they bob their entire bodies as they look for fresh water insects. But they do their prettiest dance as they hurriedly follow the foam of a receding ocean wave until a new wave comes swooshing toward them and sends them scurrying back to follow yet another wave with their high pitched "Peep-wheep." The ground robin with his alert and cheerful "Twee-eee" and the wood thrush with his soft notes at sunrise and twilight, along with the "peto-peto-peto-peto" of the tufted titmouse remind me of a living quality that reaches far beyond the hollows of their delicate air-charged bones.

The Pond

It is no fantasy of mine
To fill an indolent line
And say I am nearer my God
On Walden's grassy sod.
I am its gentle shore
And the air that trembles o'er.
In creations of my mind
Are its waters and its kind,
And at its deepest Source
My thought finds all its force.

Chapter 15
Jack's Pond

A man sits as many risks as he runs.[1]

Jack's pond has become the most important feature of all our inland lakes. It contains more acres of land than can accurately be measured. Since it is an even oval, its circumference is simple to ascertain, but its depth is immeasurable. Some say its length and breadth and depth reach from generation to generation. Yet, because it is surrounded on all four sides by man-made walls, we know that Jack, its anonymous owner, loves monotony.

All coves and inlets in Jack's pond have been "engineered" to rigidly prescribed lines. Of course these once natural bays or harbors, and even promontories, were regarded as "mistakes" on the part of Nature. For easier access to the water it was necessary to build smooth, level, and easy ports of entry.

It is self-evident that technology played a very important role in this enormous engineering triumph, since not merely motorboats, but every mechanized vehicle of transport that can maneuver on land may, at various times, be seen on its surface. Seaplanes are seen almost daily.

The submerged terrain of Jack's pond has caused endless speculation. One wonders if Jack actually owns what lies under the surface. What sort of marine life might there be? I have seen research teams with deep-diving electronic equipment floating on its surface, and I have wondered.

A WOMAN'S WALDEN

The strange thing about Jack's pond is the interaction between sun and wind. Its surface is always mirror-smooth. Significantly, one wonders if weather control has become not merely a potential, but a reality in this area of the world. The number of people drawn to it makes it an awesome possibility.

Moreover, all the animals, fish and birds in this lake evidence none of the biorhythmic characteristics of the "wild" species around my pond. These animals seem to have been genetically modified, with higher levels of intelligence, and an intuitive communication with the human beings that frequent Jack's pond. I have been reliably informed that they have been scientifically domesticated.

How could I dispute their domestication when I saw a dolphin with a box of tools strapped to his back plunge downward to an underwater diver? Fascinated, I watched until the diver surfaced with a great number of green plants protruding from an underwater carrier. As soon as he stepped ashore I asked what was the purpose of his find. He replied that on the basis of his discoveries humans would soon mass-produce underwater plants "to specification," and much of the world's hunger would be alleviated.

I have mentioned the glassy smoothness of Jack's pond, and this may account for the strange dome in its center. Those who enter this dome pay varying prices for the purpose of seeing something that lies in the heart of the pond. I began to understand why all the irregularities had been eliminated in the man-made shores that framed the pond.

It was apparent that something in the pond's depth required technological control. My curiosity grew as I watched obviously affluent, and sophisticated people enter the dome. One day a group of "experiential engineers" entered the dome, and one who had been accused of being "dome-addicted," because of his frequent visits, told me that later visitors could now control the dome-experience. This could be done by means of dials. Certain

Jack's Pond

buttons controlled lighting, and knobs labelled "preview" enabled the customers to plan their own sequences. Such sequences quickly became known as "The non-verbal convergence experience." When I asked why they were "non-verbal" a dome-initiate informed me that to see and experience what the dome had to offer left the participant so fulfilled that a verbal response was wholly superfluous.

I began to believe it was a water-theater, but an experienced participant protested violently by saying, "Of course not! A theater is a mirror of society; the dome tells us what society *will* become!" I have on occasion, when I have paced its shores, heard odd sounds escaping when the customers have held the doors open. But such sounds were too soon extinguished to be identified. They seemed to be a wired combination of human agony, guns, and bottle-smashing. However, I decided I must have been mistaken, for I saw that parents brought very small children to the dome. And why not? With such easy access to what later became known as the "Environmental Entertainment Dome," it was natural that children should not be denied entry.

Like their parents, the children became equally non-verbal. I have had such children in my classes, and while I realized that they were extremely knowledgeable there seemed no corresponding desire, or ability to use, or apply, or transmit what they knew. For the most part, their attitudes displayed either total passivity, or cynicism. Since a number of my young students were eighteen, they confessed their preference for the dome as a way of life, as education, and as a tool of government. At my shocked response, they shrugged and said, "Why not? We've had it since we were babies." One clever boy said, "We've got homogenized milk, why not homogenized government and education? We could easily have it if we made domes all over the world." When I asked if he would like the conformity classrooms this would foster, he gave a bored shrug and said, "Why not?" Persistently, I went on. "What would be the advantage in such a

A WOMAN'S WALDEN

remote control form of government?" Astutely he replied, "No one would be in charge."

But if apathetic behavior was the result in an eighteen-year-old, the opposite proved true for many of pre-school age and upward. This group suffered from a "gut" reaction to the dome experience. Apparently, selectivity in their use of the "preview" control caused them to select what was nearest to their own needs in terms of human development. Consequently they would choose the "activity" experience, since they themselves were in the active stages of growth and development. The fact that they lacked all power to separate the simulated violence of what they watched, from "real" violence meant that they became highly involved in the non-verbal dome offerings. Excitement and danger became their favorite frame of reference. The thrill of all that was illicit became their most gratifying pursuit.

It followed that dome offerings proved far stronger in the formation of their life-directions from their parents' guidance or example. They formed a society that saw all that was "illicit" as their chosen way, and from early conditioning they gravitated to terrorism, and wild, erratic orgies of violence.

Meantime, the dome offerings go on because the technology it fosters, and the scope of its offerings, grant employment to millions of people. To take it away would be tantamount to taking bread out of the mouths of families.

It becomes readily understandable that Jack's pond requires a man-made shoreline. Its undeviating regularity is perhaps the only feature that one can regard as predictable, paradoxically enclosing on its super-smooth surface a turbulence that the oceans of this world can never match.

Chapter 16
Dual Urges

We are conscious of an animal in us, which awakens in proportion as our higher nature slumbers. It is reptile and sensual, and perhaps cannot be wholly expelled; like the worms which even in life and health, occupy our bodies. Possibly we may withdraw from it, but never change its nature.... All sensuality is one though it take many forms; all purity is one. It is the same whether a man eat, or drink, or cohabit, or sleep sensually. They are but one appetite, and we only need to see a person do any one of these things to know how great a sensualist he is.[1]

As farm children we saw animals that had been slaughtered, but there proved to be a vast difference in our reactions to an already dead animal, and to our horse after it had severed an artery on a barbed wire fence. The sight of that spouting, palpitating outpouring of blood held us in a horror that brought us a steely reprimand from our father. His icily calm voice told us, "Keep quiet or leave the barn." Transfixed into pillars of salt, we were unable to move away from the horror, and equally unable to endure it; yet our endurance was silent and deeply felt.

Unlike the children of today who ask, "How can you tell if something is dead or alive?" we had no problem with the world of "real or pretend." Our eyes were not inundated with pictures of

A WOMAN'S WALDEN

killing and death in the space of one minute, and a smiling girl selling shampoo in the next sixty-second time slot. To the farm family, butchering was a necessary ritual, a part of the struggle for survival. To the city family of today a different form of "butchering" is a daily routine. Human beings are murdered on television by killers who look as normal and as real as mommy and daddy. But violence with weapons involves no physical pain; it is merely a way to solve problems between the "good guys" and the "bad guys."

One need only pause and listen to children divide themselves in their play. A frequent shout of "Now it's our turn to be the 'bad guys,' " is commonly heard. A strange reversal has taken place in the world of "make-believe." Once upon a time children longed to be good, now it is better to be a "bad guy" than a "good guy." Nice guys finish last.

While the farm children's reactions were intensified by the command to be quiet, the immobility and lack of response in a child while he is viewing television's box-enclosed violence denies him all sense of participation. Implicit in the command to the farm children was the tacit understanding that their self-control would help a loved animal. T.V. children, on the other hand, are stimulated to react from every pore of their small, activity-prone bodies. Yet at the very moment when reaction would normally take place it is cleverly cut off by a series of food-related commercials. Salivary glands are seduced into a fast raid on the refrigerator followed by a swift run back to the next blood-curdling scene, and the isolation of the "plug-in drug."

Even from children's programs, a child is taught that people are to be manipulated through legitimate deception, slapstick humor, or brute violence. What makes it all legitimate is that eventually the "hero" gets his own way.

What happens when such children are made aware of the innate "wildness" in themselves? The same cut-off responses which led them to forage for food too often take a different

Dual Urges

direction; a "pretend" killing can become brutally "real." Newspapers will report violent attacks on total strangers; it is not farfetched to assume that such attacks represent a belated surfacing of repressed responses, which date from those impressionable early years.

As Thoreau said, "I found and still find an instinct toward a higher, or, as it is named, spiritual life, as do most men, and another toward a primitive, rank and savage one, and I reverence them both. I love the wild not less than the good."[2] I note that the word "savage" is repeated three times, and I believe that each person should discover his two instincts if only to reverence that part of himself which is, indeed, wild, ferocious, untamed, uncultivated and primitive. The person who denies this in himself has not taken the first step toward that injunction, "Know thyself."

Unfortunately, the city dweller rarely seeks to know himself through close acquaintance with Nature. This knowledge cannot be purchased in "package tours." One must have the practical, everyday experience; the holiday experience will not grant it. Indians knew this when they tied young boys to a tree and left them there alone for three days and three nights. The practice has been dismissed as a mere initiation, but it fostered a life-long awareness of self-mastery and self-sufficiency.

It was when I took my four-year-old son to the zoo on a sunny Sunday afternoon that my own ferocity came to the fore. Pausing at the monkey cages, I put peanuts in my son's little outstretched palm. I lifted him up and he, with friendly eagerness, extended his offering between the bars. In a swift jerk, I felt my son's body being pulled from my arms as the caged monkey ignored the peanuts and, with incredible strength, tried to pull the little hand and arm into the cage. An instinctive and ferocious surge of resistance welled up in me as I pulled my son away. I became conscious of an instinct I had never guessed I was capable of, for in that moment I could have killed. Had the "embryo man" in

A WOMAN'S WALDEN

me merely slumbered until a proper object baited it? I can rationalize the rise of that killing instinct in myself through data which says that a mother's tendency to protect her child is stronger than all other tendencies. But such rationalizing does not cover the many times that anger, or the animal self, awakens in me with far less provocation.

Living in the same house of flesh is the other, higher or spiritual instinct. Is this why I enjoy the airy abandonment of birds? I take to myself the Psalmist's line, "Oh, that I had wings like a dove!"[3] There is a downy cushion of clouds through which I would fly, certain currents of air whose carrying powers I would like to test. When I see a bird in the branches of a tree, or on top of some light pole, or inches above an ocean wave, or in the niche of a mountain's face, I long to share their air-borne ease and freedom. I dismiss it as an "escape wish." Does it arise from a desire to live life with more spontaneity? At the same time, if I were given the freedom of a bird, would the laws of flight that govern a bird's life set in motion other and different "escape wishes"? Can freedom and abandonment become, paradoxically, a fascination and a snare? Is not my very wish "the rattling of the chain"?

In both instincts, I see the old dilemma. "For to will is present with me; but how to perform that which is good I find not. For the good that I would, I do not; but the evil which I would not, that I do."[4]

I see that the birds who fly are no more free than I am. Their spheres of flight are achieved by the "law" of their natures. To do other than fly would be an impossibility. Similarly, there can be no agreement, or temporary suspension between the two "laws" which operate in my sentient self, and the higher self, or what we call the soul. "There is never an instant's truce between virtue and vice."[5] We may grow indifferent to our own internal warfare; we may try to ignore it, and repress it, and many deny altogether that it exists, but if we deny its existence we deceive no one except ourselves. I return to Paul who

Dual Urges

describes his two warring natures as slavery. "I am carnal, sold under sin."[6]

What is termed a savage instinct, St. Paul calls his "fleshly" nature. Who, then, are the servants of that owner? Our five senses, chiefly those of appetite. As has been said, "all sensuality is one, though it take many forms; all purity is one. It is the same whether a person eat, or drink, or cohabit, or sleep sensually. They are but one appetite, and we only need to see a person do any *one* of these things to know how great a sensualist he is. The impure can neither stand nor sit with purity. When the reptile is attacked at one mouth of his burrow, he shows himself at another. If you would be chaste, you must be temperate. What is chastity? How shall a man know if he is chaste? He shall not know it."[7]

If these are the natural inclinations to which we are forever bound, what is there to "reverence" in them? I will begin with what seems most harmless, eating. Yet it is that to which I am truly a "slave." The very thoughts in my mind, that process by which I approach God, must of necessity draw their sustenance from my last meal. Therefore nothing can defile my "higher instincts" through food. Did not Christ himself say, "There is nothing from without that can defile a man?"[8] Then what is it in my appetite for food which reveals the extent of my sensuality in all other areas where purity and impurity are weighed? I see that it lies in the hidden consent and inner devotion which my "higher instincts" give to food. More, I see from this why it is better to "live low and fare hard."[9] In professing to "love the wild not less than the good,"[10] we are giving tacit recognition to the bodily instincts as the "temple" or channel through which the highest realities are transmuted.

The very appetite which is betrayed by a swollen abdomen reveals our mind's devotion to the maggot's level of gluttony. It is not difficult to understand why Dante, in his vision of hell, placed gluttons on a lower, and more disgusting level than the sexual sinners. The life-force by which we are all brought to being is

A WOMAN'S WALDEN

transgressed with less evil than our physical appetites for food. How can this be? Sex may result in the birth of a child, but the offal and excretions in which Dante placed the gluttons was a graphic picture of the results of over-eating. Moreover, the perfection of Dante's metaphor is clearly revealed in Cerberus, the three-headed dog, who illustrates our complicated human trinity of body, mind, and spirit all concentrated on food.

How earnestly should the preservation of the "higher or poetic" faculties be pursued? We do it by abstaining "from much food of any kind."[11] To be captivated and dominated by eating as a natural and essential function of our lives implies a willingness to be servants of other sensualities as well.

I can understand why Christ told His disciples, with regard to their failure in casting out a specific demon: "This kind goeth not out but by prayer and fasting."[12] As surely as we must crawl before we can walk, we must deal with sensual impurity on its most seemingly innocent level. And where does personal self-discipline and personal *self-directedness* seem most innocuous, if not where eating is concerned? I wish it could be inscribed in every home, "From exertion comes wisdom and purity; from sloth, ignorance and sensuality."[13]

What specific *exertion* do I exercise in abstaining from food? Ah—the first entrance to mind is through the gateway of an appetizing fragance, the odor of food in my nostrils. Next, there is the desire aroused by the sight of food; both of these wonderful senses activate my salivary glands to the extent that I can actually taste by anticipation that which I am about to eat. When I struggle to deny these natural urges by fasting, am I weakened? Yes, if in addition to smelling, tasting, seeing, I have spent a day at coarse and heavy labor. Long labor compels me to eat as heavily as I have labored, but in the normal exertion that grants my mind an exhilarating command over the external senses, my thoughts are liberated from other distractions in the contemplation of divine things. It is in this sense that my *whole*

Dual Urges

being, my *entire self*, is given over to a higher pursuit.

Does this give me the right to boast of self-conquest? What about the danger of a more mental temptation? An egotistical sense of superiority? Simply to speak of such an exertion implies, "Aha! See what I have done!" The pharisaical self-congratulation is there: "God, I thank thee that I am not as other men."[14] But if the exertion is real it is followed by St. Paul's, "I [now] know that in me dwelleth no good thing."[15] When good actions are produced in us by a power not our own, we advance at once away from the triumph over the senses to that more subtle, secretive, and pervasive temptation to pride, the "queen of sins."

By easy stages I am taught that real self-conquest is actually a yielding of my ordinary inclinations to God. At the same time, as I give in to God's call for purity, I have to have enough self-knowledge to turn over to His control all that I cannot reach by my own efforts. In spite of this, there is pleasure that far transcends self-complacency in conquering our several instincts. When we consciously grapple with the power of our instinctual drives, we do not merely repress our sensuality, we find a substitute activity which utilizes all the force of our raw and "savage wildness" in such a way that the "higher self" is gratified. The fact that social demands are also met is less important than the satisfaction of our "inner man," which recognizes the substitute activity as a cooperative act. The double urge, by which all men are afflicted, finds in substitution that neither inclination is opposed. Rather, there is a fusion and harmony which harnesses all the fire of the senses so that both the animal self and the spiritual self achieve a very necessary reward. Surely this is what St. Paul meant when he said, "I keep under my body, and bring it into subjection."[16] It is only as the inner self-mastery is gained that the needs of our fellow humans can be served.

The imagery of fishing is very apropos here. I shall let my "mind descend into my body and redeem it, and treat myself

A WOMAN'S WALDEN

with ever-increasing respect."[17] But besides this mental fishing I discover that I have always been a female carpenter. Long before the so-called women's liberation movement, I was a builder. My materials? The "temple" of my own flesh and blood.

Chapter 17
The "Smoke-Self"

Be a Columbus to whole new continents and worlds within you, opening new channels, not of trade, but of thought.[1]

One day, when the fog was so thick I could not see either the pond or the houses across the street, I remembered Thomas Merton's reference to a "smoke-self." Watching the heavy fog, I was glad there was no need to drive through it, or hang over it in an airplane, unable to land, because not even precision instruments could pierce those furry, grey mists. Yet, in terms of an individual lifetime, it would be far worse to be lost in a concept of myself that would vanish as fog vanishes.

As I see it, a "smoke-self" is created in role responses to certain circumstances and social interaction. To take these as indications of the real person is to build one's concept on variables and fluctuations. In the search for identity, social involvement takes on the attributes of fog, since they are based on externals we can never clearly see. The most fog-enshrouded conclusions about the self are those which fasten on "what others will think." Unfortunately, public opinion polls tell us that even our leaders are in fact evaluated by this same criterion, and policies are changed as a result of overwhelming public opinion. This being so, the true definition of democracy is perhaps "mobocracy."

But if I would know myself, my actual identity can never be

A WOMAN'S WALDEN

built on the self-image given me through social feedback, still less on the wish to make a good impression. We do not need to "run amok" against society so much as we need to allow society, rather, *invite* society to run against us. In the search for authenticity it will be impossible to avoid social confrontation of one sort or another.

How then shall we learn to know ourselves? "Not till we are lost, in other words, not till we have lost the world do we begin to find ourselves, and realize where we are and the infinite extent of our relations."[2]

Does this suggest a retreat from the world, and a reflective solitude in which we contemplate that tiredly over-used object, our navel? Between extreme withdrawal and my need for genuine "personhood," what alternatives exist? Unless contemplation can strengthen me for obedience to an inner dynamic by which all things exist in a diversity of forms I will have no contact with it, since diversity of form does not imply imperfection but uniqueness, or individuality. Clearly, the diversity of forms in Nature cannot help me. My dog has no such problem, since he is what he was created. My orange tree was not consulted about its orange-tree-ness, but the more oranges it bears the more it declares its uniqueness. Among them all, I alone can choose.

As I exercise my freedom of choice I can allow others to dictate my reactions, my obligations, my values in a misguided sense of doing my "duty." In this context I may be a wife, mother, teacher, consumer, tax-payer, church member, political activist, business woman, yet none of these functions, nor their aggregate, contain my whole identity. They exist as separate experiences with a different constellation of love, honor, power and knowledge attached to each function. They are like "bandages" which make me visible to society, as if the real person were contained in social involvement.

The other choice is withdrawal; not an escape, but a condition

The "Smoke-Self"

which has been described as a polarity. In dealing with polarities, I will have to come to terms with two contradictions in myself. One is that habit of thinking that can be defined in a series of social actions, as if life consisted in experiences that would grant me either responsibility or guilt. The second contradiction is the idea that life is often lived more fully when we drastically reduce our doings, seeings, range of hearing, tasting and experiencing. The car that takes me sixty miles an hour may bring me to places I have never seen, but I shall not see them better for being shown them in a blur of speed. Between these two polarities my own ambivalence is created.

At a certain stage in life we embrace as many roles as appeal to us, eager for the benefits attached. We are unaware that a multiplicity of roles and benefits will dull our sensibilities. Yet if I choose withdrawal will I be equal to the emptiness or the "desert" experience which is the well-known by-product of self-denial? If I deliberately deprive myself of a status-quo existence, resisting all social and economic pressures to conform, will I not be working against a true selfhood? What distinctions or renunciations must I make in order to maintain a healthy tension between the demands of my inner self and the demands of society? In a temporary retreat from social involvements, will I not find when I return that I am better equipped to translate the self-discipline that such a withdrawal demands into a more discriminating, effectual social interaction?

But for one who has allowed society and environment to dictate his choices, nothing is more difficult than a full retreat. Merely to do less than he has done before will involve an entirely new capacity for simplification that may well be beyond his powers. Our ambivalence as to whether our selfhood lies in "what others will think," or whether selfhood is found in thoughtful withdrawal, sets up a divided heart. It follows that a recognition of our divided selves is the necessary first step toward a simpler, more deliberate, less confused way of life.

A WOMAN'S WALDEN

In order to awaken myself to a new order of selfhood I cannot give myself to a change that takes place in my thinking alone. To translate the recognition of my divided self into a simplified, inner-directed life requires more than thoughtful admission. More than my intellect must be involved if such thinking is not to grow into a deformity in my personality, for "conscience [thinking] doth make cowards of us all"[3] unless it is "digested" into actions. If I reduce my activities and attempt a withdrawal that revolves around some vague idea of self-improvement, my attempt will inevitably fail. Why? Because without the winnowing agency of the bread-and-potatoes concerns of life, my thinking can too easily turn into "castles" of delusion. Hidden behind the search for the authentic self are dangers of fantasy that must *earn* their validity in a world of conflicting and contradictory values. As I cannot live by bread—or dollars—alone, it is equally true that I cannot live entirely in the inner world of my thoughts. They are opposites which must balance each other out.

Paradoxically, I live most deeply when my actions alternate between doing less and doing nothing. Will stillness, leisure and rest bring on a vacancy that will soon be tenanted by "legions" of evil? Yes. Vacancy and emptiness pose real dangers. Though it is a cliché to say that nothing can exist in a vacuum, withdrawal requires a dynamic without which it can, and often does, descend to "dionysian" levels. We are like the man of the Gadarenes. All the multiple activities that make us a torment to ourselves differ little from the wounds this man inflicted on himself. It was only at the approach of an invisible Power that this man could be brought to see his *need* for help. Was he willing to be helped? No. Help was met with resistance and the cry of his tormentors, "What have we to do with you?" Like this man, I am bound by my several role-involvements which speak as realistically as "Legion" spoke for the man of the Gadarenes. These say *for* me, "I have her in my possession; do not prevent me from

The "Smoke-Self"

accomplishing my mission which is to possess and devour her energies."

Is this a parable of disorder? Not necessarily. Christ's use of the word "Legion" suggests regimental forces, among them principalities, powers and rulers. If these prove to be no threat there are other means of self-destruction, as in the parable.

How was this man's emptiness filled? He received a commission, a single obligation. Jesus told him: "Go home to thy friends, and tell them how great things the Lord hath done for thee."[4] Where once this man's identity was merged and controlled by a "legion" of evil spirits, his friends were shocked to find him "in his right mind." Like him we, too, are restored when the deepest needs of our inward selves are in harmony with God and our practical, everyday lives.

There is no single technique, no single school of meditation, no single order of contemplation that can bring us to such a point. Our retreat from the "world" of our commitments must be done for us by the "Spirit of Promise." For, "we have received not the spirit of the world, but the spirit which is of God; that we might *know* the things that are freely given to us of God."[5] Therefore our original separation from "legion" possession is done *for* us by a Power not our own. But that is not to say that we can see with full clarity the roads that lie ahead for us.

Yet there *is* a *rest* provided for anxiety with regard to self-direction. After the Spirit of Promise has made us aware of our futile involvements, and even after our inward selves are in harmony with our practical, everyday lives, and after we are no longer possessed by our tormenting "legions," our normal desires and motives continue to operate. We need guidance. For this I accept myself as a blind person. "I will bring the blind by a way that they knew not; I will lead them in paths they have not known: I will make darkness light before them, and crooked things straight. These things will I do unto them, and not forsake them."[6] Here, also, the emphasis is *not* on our own actions, but on God's actions on our behalf.

But beautiful as they are, such words are no more than rhetoric unless they correspond with my free decisions in the ordinary affairs of life. In the events of my own life, my inner self must recognize the intervention of a higher *will* than my own, and a higher level of pardon than I can extend to myself. How much of an "authentic self" can I know in my self-divided heart, if all my energies are dissipated in self-serving pursuits? If all the hours of an ordinary day, and the thoughts of such a day, contain no thoughts focused on God, then I cannot *expect* His guidance for, "As [a man] thinketh in his heart, so is he."[7] It is self-identity of this sort that removes me from everything my *natural* self is fastened upon, until my very thinking is *one* with my living.

The first to be affected by such a reversal will be my approaches to ambition, money, pride and "all the hungers that exhaust my nature with their bleeding."[8] In brief, I must "die" to every effort I have ever attempted in my struggle to know myself. Above all, I must "die" to that "narcissistic dialogue" that too often passes for self-analysis. I "die" also to those slogans I have caught from the age in which I live. Here I do not speak of metaphysical or metaphorical death, but that inner disunity which is a living death, since to be human is to be both body and soul.

"Living becomes then the constant adjustment of thought to life and life to thought in such a way that we are always growing, always experiencing new things in the old and old things in the new. Thus life is always new."[9] In such a unity of my divided self, I learn that I find my self-identity in losing it in self-surrender to God.

But "self-surrender to God" sounds glib in the writing. It is too pat. It can be spoken with too much ease. And such "surrenders" often fill us with enthusiasm, too often followed by a false sense of security. We grow proud of the experience itself and walk about with a false sense of superiority, much like the offensive bumper

The "Smoke-Self"

stickers which read, "I found it," as if faith were a matter of keeping up with the Joneses and by implication saying, "See how much better I am than you are."

For this reason "self-surrender" to God is never a "once-only" affair. It calls for continual *re*-surrender. As changes and new developments take place in our lives, an early experience of "saying yes to God" loses some of its intensity and with loss comes doubt. Was it real? Was it valid? Why do I feel nothing now? Time and change and distance and decay have come between that long ago "yes." We learn there is nothing final in any decision. What happens then? A new cycle forms and we return like children to the source of our first comfort, finding there wheels within wheels within wheels within wheels—

A WOMAN'S WALDEN

"Neither From Nor Towards"

Why hide what is?
Why separate the *be* of being
From its doing? Do!
Deny the tyranny of self
In duties done.

Why die to self?
A stern decree declares
The way of death brings life,
And hammer blows designed
To crush the flame
Makes self assert its strength
And multiplies its sparks.

Self slain by self lives on:
"The mind will not obey the mind."
Divided into *be* and *do?*
Where doing seeks the nod
Of priests' approval?
And that poor core of *being*
Is dressed in outward deeds
Chameleon clad?

My never-dying heart dies not
For all such breakings,
But wears its living colors still. More!
It renders every act of self-willed doing
Deeds of deadness,
Prophecies and knowledge, passing fair
But passing:
A body "burned" by Sinai's cold command.

Yet one small heart-begotten moment
Past death, past reasoned thought lives on,
And with its Kingly crimson
Covers all.

—Ruthe T. Spinnanger

Chapter 18
Symbolic Activities

I hearing get, who had but ears,
And sight, who had but eyes before,
I moments live, who had but years,
And truth discern, who knew but learning's lore.[1]

It cannot be said that I began building when I contracted to have my Woman's Walden house constructed. I began building before I was out of my cradle. The motion of that first cradle's wheel was my introduction to the wheel of providence, and the spoke that was uppermost in infancy was soon at the bottom of all. Change quickly introduced me to change. From my early recognition of inconstancy I became a builder, perhaps in an attempt to leave my own mark of constancy on the landscape of variation. To change things became a way of perfecting them. Not that I ever succeeded.

What do I seek when I work in wood, or marble, or earth, or ink? Why does change direct me to search for perfection? For that matter, what is perfection? I learn that it is a rendering of several Hebrew and Greek words containing the basic idea of completeness. Then it is not simply change which makes builders of us, but a recognition that things around us are incomplete. In our infant ways we try to change our surroundings. We build our sand castles and walk away while the surf erases them. We learn with childish grief that we, ourselves, are incomplete, and we reach out to our parents for assurance. For a short while we draw a sense of completeness from that first trinity of mother-father-child, yet growth and adulthood in no way lessens our search for completeness.

We use a wide variety of "building materials" in our search for perfection. At first, everything centers around our early skills. Our materials are the abstract terms of would-should-should-not, for which, as we act in a manner suitable to our age, we earn the accolades of esteem and excellence. We begin to understand what is required of us, and we learn to give the "perfect" answer. We present our perfectly finished assignments, only to find there is more to that sense of completeness. We learn that the perfect rose, the perfect copy, the perfect object, though "faultily faultless" are not the perfections we are seeking.

Meanwhile, the wheel of providence turns inexorably round, and after innumerable turnings we pause to consider with Job "the balancings of the clouds," and see them as "the wonderful workings of One who is perfect in knowledge. With whom there is no variableness, neither shadow of turning."[2]

Was our attempt to rebuild and reshape our own abilities, our own things, our own places, our own times, our own persons merely a failing effort to remind ourselves of the need for partaking of that supreme perfection? Were all my efforts, symbolical attempts to reach what lies forever beyond me? Was my very life saying, "Change and decay in all around I see? Oh, Thou Who changest not, abide with me?"[3] And so I grasped at the relative perfection of God's works, instead of entering that building not made with hands.

My sand castles had, at long last, led me to the Rock upon which I could build my house of faith, in which I could find myself "complete in Christ." Yes, that house was "lofty enough to create some obscurity overhead, where flickering shadows play at evening about the rafters."[4]

But for a long time I was prevented from entering my house of faith because, until I learned that faith was more than "soul force," I looked at my emotions, my feelings, my opinions, and my convictions for verification. Faith was no mere myth that I could dismiss as inexpressible; nor was it an interior, subjective thing separated from all externals.

Paradoxically, my act of belief began with intellectual consent at the very moment when my reason admitted that it could do nothing to prove the actuality of God. My assent went beyond my reason's reasoned evidence, and I was left without my usual "mode of knowing." Like the person who says, "I don't know why I am doing this," I saw that I was going against all reason and acting from the heart. What happened? I saw that my reason was not repressed, or denied, or frustrated; rather, it was pacified by Pascal's conviction, "The heart has its reasons which the reason cannot know." My mind rested, and rests, in loving God.

But faith is more than a "yes" to Scripture, or to any statement *about* God. Statements, being composed of words, have led to differences in human interpretation and to human interactions which have placed horrible stains on the tapestry of faith. Beautiful and persuasive as the words may be, they are no more than channels through which I am brought to peace *in* God.

As Thomas Merton says, "The known and the unknown overlap.... The unknown remains unknown. It is still a mystery, for it cannot cease to be one. The function of faith is not to reduce mystery to rational clarity, but to integrate the unknown and the known together in a living whole, in which we are more and more able to transcend the limitations of our external self."[5]

However, when I saw how many mansions there were in the household of faith, and how many solicitations call the believer to become submerged in their religious machinery, I became concerned for the anonymity that any mass-movement fosters. In spite of the ecumenical movement, large segments of the church deny the individual her personal freedom and growth in Christ.

A WOMAN'S WALDEN

Too many groups are held together by subtle forms of spiritual superiority.

A peculiarly virulent form of the "numbers" racket has invaded evangelical circles, to the extent that the unchurched soon become disillusioned by the "head-count" approach to faith. Newspapers, with their understandable need for statistics, will publicize the fact that eight hundred would-be converts "went forward" for conversion or renewal. Nothing is said about the *mechanical aids* to these altar-call migrations, or the behind-the-scenes programming of zealous church workers instructed to rise en masse on cue in order to give courage to the "lost."

As with politics, so with religion, the end justifies the means. It is said, with much accuracy, that if even one "soul" is brought through to faith, the operation is justified. Can we quarrel with such rationales, in view of the enormous "cost" of that *one* Calvary?

But when such campaigns draw to themselves huge sums of money in which prestigious foundations become virtual tax shelters, and the poor are left to the mercy of government subsidies, the first requirement of true faith is no longer met. "A new commandment I give unto you, that ye love one another."[6] And where should first love (that love which is not kindled by human means) spend itself? Our first obligation is to need, and to one's nearest, which is also the law of spiritual ecology.

It is easy to quote, "He that loveth father or mother more than me is not worthy of me."[7] On that basis scores have neglected their immediate families with the grandiloquent gesture of serving God.

Example: A mother of six small children saw her priority in service to God as a "call" to use her very real leadership abilities in church work. Nearly every evening of the week, nightly meals became a tense, clock-watching interval in which the atmosphere spoke louder than words. "Mommy can't be late" destroyed the sacramental realities of the family meal. (If Christ "was made known of them in breaking of bread,"[8] should not our human

Symbolic Activities

sharing be equally solemn?) Ignored and seldom heard in connection with the divine "call" is that parallel injunction, "if any that provide not for his own . . . is worse than an infidel."[9]

Where spiritual energy is concerned, human ecology should alert us to the "roots" of our problem. As people, we are not numbers, neither are we merely souls. As to the first, we are not mechanical digits, but individuals. As for the designation "lost souls," this refers to what is, in fact, a portion of our total personhood here on earth, and ignores that "temple" of the soul, which is the body, the holy container of our earthly life. We should not be depersonalized into that ultimate of our self-hood: soul. Until death arrives, our souls should not, and cannot, be separated from our bodies; we are, therefore, persons.

In spite of the fact that we are socially-oriented beings, spiritual growth cannot be limited to mass movements, or "the assembling of ourselves together," necessary as corporate worship is. In the crowd, even in a spiritual crowd, we lose our spiritual perspective, and turn into spiritual chameleons, taking on values that are not our own. Too often, conformity to the group is mistaken for spiritual re-birth, when it is in reality no more than a yielding to prevailing opinions.

How shall we know that we have not followed "prevailing opinions"? Just as those first followers had their wilderness wanderings in the desert before entering their promised land, so we too much accept what often appears to be a delay. Whatever else it may have been, the Israelites' forty years were a time when they were alone with their God. Are we concerned about the genuineness of our relationship with God? It can only be proved to us as we are "alone with the Alone."

But even if we reject the desert experience as so much historical data, we are still faced with Christ's command. "When thou prayest, enter into thy closet . . . and thy Father which seeth in secret shall reward thee openly."[10] It is the perspective of the "secret place," which can only be known in solitude, that urges us

A WOMAN'S WALDEN

to seek stillness and aloneness with God. It is the *one* condition by which we can *know* God. "Be *still* and know that I am God."[11]

It is the desert experience and the *deliberate* pursuit of stillness that fits us for our nearest service to our fellow humans. As I see it, that is best fulfilled in the unplanned encounter. Such circumstances bring about most naturally the one-to-one sharing, the spontaneous gesture of hospitality in which common elements are served, and where the everyday truths of our existence are laid bare. Until we have learned to love our own solitude in independence of the opinions of others, we have nothing unique to share with others; all is nothing more than a hodge-podge of warmed up left-overs.

I have said that my house is beautiful, but I have not told you why. Is it perhaps because it makes no attempt to *be* beautiful? I have called it my "bought-and-prayed-for house," and the result is not a *paid*-for house. It is an immensely satisfying suggestion of aims that go beyond mere house*keeping*. In it I have achieved a "sort of lower heaven overhead . . . A house whose inside is as open and manifest as a bird's nest, and you cannot go in at the front door and out the back without seeing some of its inhabitants; where to be a guest is to be presented the freedom of the house, and not be carefully excluded from seven-eighths of it, shut up in a particular cell, and told to make myself at home there, . . . in solitary confinement . . . where hospitality is the art of keeping you at the greatest distance."[12]

Indoors, I have noticed that none of my guests can remain long in what we refer to as the "living room." The architectural openness of my house suggests freedom, and the pond never fails to draw people to the rear of the house. Of course they pause to marvel at the actual bird's nest no more than twelve inches from my front door. Two coral footed mourning doves have made a nest in the very center of my hanging fern. At first someone said, "How picturesque of you to put a fake bird in your fern!" At my shocked protest, she went on, "But it does not move!" I realized

Symbolic Activities

with sorrow in my heart that my guest had a penchant for fake birds, and so I frightened our little mother away from her nest. (One needed only to open the mailbox, which we stopped using after that.) Since then we have had the advent of twins, and not even the clicking of my camera at close range has frightened either mother or father away. They have come to a house of peace. I must remember to ask an ornithologist whether our organ music may have been a factor in bringing them here. At precisely ten A.M. the male bird relieves the female and when she does not get back by four P.M. we hear his plaintive, "loo, loo, loo." Except for size, there seems little difference in the nurturing capacity of either male or female. In late afternoon they will often remain together in the nest conferring about their babies' food, which we see the little ones take from deep in the parent bird's throat, warm and pre-digested.

Too many of our "tract houses" (and mine is a tract house), resemble enlarged boxes or prophetic coffins. it is clear that straight lines and utility, or economy for profit, express the pragmatism of this dollar democracy. If I were a surveyor, I would make my observations, first of all, from the air, there to learn the beauty of irregularity and curved lines. What welcome relief one finds, when viewing the patchwork squares of our country from an airplane, to see straight, man-made lines broken by the willfully meandering curves of a river, or a swathe of contour plowing.

I am certain that the upright walls of my house were made more acceptable to me by the broken roof line which unexpectedly rounds itself outward. It is as if its mass-producing designer had let his pen slide beyond the designated squares in an impatient ellipsis—like this: ⌒ . That curve is supported by two scrolls of lacy, grape-leafed wrought iron. The eye is given a restful interval of relief from the straight outlines of walls and windows by the wavy iron lines.

As for hospitality, my life is not remote from its symbols, nor

A WOMAN'S WALDEN

shall my professional life ever divorce me from my kitchen. That would be to substitute words for deeds; I have found no theoretical replacement for actions. I have returned full circle to the simple foods of my childhood. Moreover, the herbs drying from the old well-hook in my modern kitchen are not so much clutter as they are the evidence that my eating and drinking are related to an organic impulse that no pre-packaged bread or drink can give me. All the human hand shapes, however crude, is endowed with a spiritual force.

But for one who would move beyond the restrictions of our "social obligation" level of hospitality, it is well to imitate the poor of this world, who with simple belief in the chain reactions of a good deed, believe that "a cup of cold water only shall in no wise lose its reward." The wisdom that framed that line must have recognized our money-oriented mentality, since it appeals to us on the level of our innate self-interest. "Give, and it shall be given unto you; good measure, pressed down, and shaken together, and running over, shall men give into your bosom. For with the same measure that ye mete withal [large or small] it shall be measured to you again."[13]

Does this place all our giving on the level of exchange or barter? By no means. I would rather invite to my house those who have no means of returning my invitation. Widows and fatherless are first on my guest list, lest I forget the *in*voluntary poverty that once was mine, and that stern maxim: "Only the poor can feel for the poor."

Perhaps it may seem strange that my favorite guest was one to whom I never issued an invitation. Yet ours is a harmony of opposites. He does not fit into that well-known stereotype, first a guest, then a burden, then a pest. Nor is he one of those jovial back-slapping, easy-to-know sorts; nor is he one whom you esteem and honor by reason of fame rather than familiarity. True, there was nothing in either his appearance or his possessions that would give him the "accepted" qualifications for social exchange.

Symbolic Activities

Those who consider themselves superior to him say that he lacks intellect. They say that he does not clothe his thoughts in the elegance that superiority demands. He is not polite to the point where he avoids giving offense. Indeed, some say he is most tactless where his own best interests are concerned.

When I try to describe him, the first things I note are his compelling eyes, and his large construction worker's hands. No, he is not self-employed; he has always worked for others, and never at a union wage. He hangs around with men of decidedly questionable reputations. Once he attracted a huge crowd by defending a woman taken in adultery. His defense was by way of a question which diverted the abusive crowd and dispersed them. After that he was regarded as "one of them."

When he came to my door, I had no intention of making him a permanent guest. His first words were these: "I think you remember me." I replied, "I am certain that I have never met you before," and I was about to close the door. Something in his manner stopped me as he reminded me of little Jack, a child I had once taken into my home until he grew up. Very quietly he said, "I was that little child. I was hungry and thirsty and you gave me food and drink. As you have done it to the least of these, you have done it unto Me."[14]

A WOMAN'S WALDEN

Tribute to a Baby Bird

How far from what it will be
Is the featherless baby bird.
The open beak
Now larger than its wings,
A tottering head
That awkwardly sustains
Its own wide open jaws.
Raw, new-made need
That gives no forward glimpse
Of radiant plumage
Or of will-be flights.

For this the mother bird
Flies tirelessly from food to nest,
For this unpretty tribute
Weak and wide-mouthed faith.
Bird patience
In a patterned miniature of God,
When needs like these
Unfeathered, wide-beaked birds
Reflect for us
Our groaning emptiness,
Our cries which are no more
Than bird, or child-like
Trustful asking.

Reprinted from
Christianity Today

Chapter 19
Summer Locked Up

Thought secures its own conditions, . . . It is true, we are such poor navigators that our thoughts for the most part, stand off and on upon a harborless coast, are conversant only with the bights and bays of poesy, or steer for the public ports of entry, and go into the dry docks of science, where they merely refit for this world, and no natural currents concur to individualize them.[1]

It must not be thought that because no ice forms in Walden III in Florida that a change of season does not take place. I learn from a nearby botanist that there is no plant which does not "sleep" for certain periods of the year. I see a sluggish greyness which the cold, grey rain brings to the surface of the pond. The sun moves daily to the left of where I stand, and appears shrouded in many layers of grey mist. At such times the water that brings heaven to my feet cannot contain its usual profile because the author and finisher of that reflection has withdrawn.

The winter solstice brings a period of heavy rain, so heavy that no visitor ventures out. Indoors, there is a sense of snug coziness, yet I miss the silence of the snow and the sense of home enfolded in snowdrifts over and above the windows, as they were in North Dakota.

Here, the heavy sheeted rain is like an insistent voice which will not be ignored. The pond rises visibly. If I knew all the laws of

A WOMAN'S WALDEN

Nature what would I infer from that particular result? How do I relate it to the ethics of my own life? I claim that, as the rain secures its own conditions, the sum total of life's circumstances similarly have an emphasis that cannot be measured except where they direct the inclinations, watered by my thoughts, which secure their own conditions. ". . . That which was at first but an inclination in the shore in which a thought was harbored becomes an individual lake, cut off from the ocean, . . . changes perhaps, from salt water to fresh becomes a sweet sea, dead sea, or a marsh."[2]

> *It is the law of the average. Such a rule of the two diameters not only guides us toward the sun in the system and the heart in man, but draw lines through the length and breadth of the aggregate of a man's particular daily behaviors and waves of life into his coves and inlets, and where they intersect will be the height and depth of his character. Perhaps we need only to know how his shores trend and his adjacent country or circumstance to infer his depth and concealed bottom. If he is surrounded by mountainous circumstances, an Achillean shore, whose peaks overshadow and are reflected in his bosom, they suggest a corresponding depth in him, but a low and smooth shore prove him shallow on that side.*[3]

But where do I find the "natural currents" by which to "navigate" my thoughts? I want to avoid "the public ports of entry." If Emerson is correct, my thoughts will be directed by a "natural magnetism which is sure to select what belongs to it." In another context, I am glad to note in that remark the absence of struggle.

My pond teaches me the same lesson. Without exertion or effort, without inlet or outlet, it responds to rain, sun, evaporation

Summer Locked Up

and its own concealed fountain. All its fluctuations remove no more than its outer skin. It is activated by a higher law and higher thoughts than mine. Yet neither the pond, nor the birds, nor plants, nor the trees have been granted the gift of words. Of course they speak, and "there is no speech nor language where their voice is not heard."[4] Yet I sometimes think this extension of natural abilities in man is a stumbling block in the navigation of our thoughts. Have we allowed the consciousness of other people, their practices, opinions, and reactions and interactions to determine both the direction of our thoughts and our inclinations? If our outward deeds are done in response to social pressures then we are truly little different than machines.

Again, we are not inanimate stones, all but impervious to influence. No, we are more like the pond in that we can no more refuse to receive the "rain" that falls, as we live and move in the orbit of social machinery. To find our own thoughts we must consent to a "winter" of solitude. Our ears must be closed, first and foremost, to market-place values. "Getting and spending we lay waste our powrs."[5] The process must begin with self-knowledge, self-discovery and self-acceptance, which is the essence of self-love. But this is not the self-love of personal advantage. The "winter" of solitude is not chosen in order to freeze all fellow feeling, or to reduce personal understanding to a private function.

Like winter itself, it is a period in which to listen for an inner silence. It is a time in which to separate the distant from the near at hand; to reflect, if you please, on the allegory of a cake of ice. "Perhaps the blue color of water and ice is due to the light and air they contain, and the most transparent is the bluest."[6] If the "light" inside of self is darkness, how great is that darkness! As the light in a cake of ice is more discernible than the light in plain water, so does a solitary season in human life bring us back the source of all Light. As the cake of ice is separated from its liquid state, a person in solitude is removed from social engulfment, and

A WOMAN'S WALDEN

is no longer submerged in society's tensions, prejudices, violence, technology and materialism.

Is it an escape? By no means. It is a seasonal retreat; a rest from the heat of the day. It *is* "summer locked up." It is a time to stand back and regain a true perspective, which is impossible when we crowd together like so many buckets of putrid water. "Why is it that a bucket of water soon becomes putrid, but frozen remains sweet forever? It is commonly said that this is the difference between the affections and the intellect."[7] Solitude and a "winter" silence are the only ways in which we can internalize Christ's statement, "Behold, I make all things new."[8]

In constant association and multipled encounters with people our capacity for caring is deadened. We are acted upon; we do not act, we react. Finally, we grow numb and submit to our homogenized loss of selfhood. It is out of over-exposure to people that genuine loneliness grows, for to choose solitude is not to choose loneliness. Rightly understood, we are "never less alone than when alone."[9]

Solitude gives us a time in which to know ourselves by our earliest preferences; as individuals rather than as an extension of a family, as a member of an ethnic group, and an affiliate of some organization. All such context views of self fuses our identity to the level of an integer: faceless, apart from our organizational grouping.

Long before old age the "winter" of solitude should be *deliberately* cultivated. Solitude will enable us to bring something besides long years to old age. We deceive ourselves if we believe the security of money lessens the frigidity that is often associated with old age. If the mind and heart are not prepared in advance with resources that go beyond the physical comforts, money will fail to provide them. We should consider, far in advance of our declining years, that if we can find no pleasure in solitude, in the company of our own selves, the length of our life will matter little. We cannot expect to be venerated in old age if

Summer Locked Up

we have had no respect for ourselves, or so little respect that we see ourselves only as mirror images in the minds of others. Solitude will teach us that, as the pond is fed by a hidden spring, so must our walled-in soul drink from secret springs. We need to look at what the eye has never seen, to rely on what is never made visible, to hope in what can never be touched. This cannot be done in the company of any human. It is the secret place of the Most High.

Chapter 20
"The Green Blade"

I am a parcel of vain strivings tied
  By a chance bond together,
Dangling this way and that, their links
  Were made so loose and wide,
    Methinks,
For milder weather.

But now I see I was not plucked for naught,
  And after in life's vase of glass
    Set while I might survive,
But by a kind hand brought
    Alive
To a strange place.

That stock thus thinned will soon redeem its hours,
  And by another year,
Such as God knows, with freer air,
  More fruits and fairer flowers
    Will bear,
While I droop here.[1]

Why is April "the cruelest month"? The days grow longer and are filled with promise, as little streams, this earth, and my own pulses all flow together in obedience to a silent law.

A WOMAN'S WALDEN

I am affected as if in a peculiar sense I stood in the laboratory of the Artist who made the world and me,— had come to where He was still at work, sporting on this bank [Walden] and with excess of energy strewing His fresh designs about. I feel as if I were nearer to the vitals of this globe . . . . No wonder that the earth expresses itself outwardly in leaves, it so labors with the idea inwardly. The atoms have already learned this law, and are pregnant by it. The overhanging leaf sees here its prototype. Internally, whether in the globe or animal body, . . . Even ice begins with delicate crystal leaves, as if it had flowed into molds which the fronds of water-plants have impressed on the watery mirror. The whole tree itself is but one leaf, and rivers are still vaster leaves whose pulp is intervening the earth, and towns and cities are the ova of insects in their axils.[2]

When I wrote earlier that Walden III was less a *place* than an experience, I wrote in ignorance of what simplicity, and solitude, and stillness would bring me. I was guilty of thinking "bounds are henceforth set to our lives and our fates decided."[3] What a relief to find it is not so. The self I was, and the self I have become in the space of one year, shows me that life has possibilities far wider than my view of it can conceive. Like yourself, I find I cannot be extravagant enough in recognizing this fact. It reaches "exceeding abundantly above all that we ask or think."[4]

But distance and detachment were part of the price to be paid. One cannot claim to love the abstractions of the simplified life. Simplicity without a genuine withdrawal from cities, shopping centers, and superficial encounters with people remains no more than wishful thinking.

I am writing this in a "cathedral" of very tall pine trees behind a church in my neighborhood. I long for another, wilder place, perhaps in New England, but the need to hear trees breathe

"The Green Blade"

above my head, and to walk on brown paths of pine-scented needles is one that should not be denied to anyone. Mere travel cannot grant it. Every village in America, as well as every city, should have its wilderness retreat within walking distance of every home, so that the unplanned need, that seasonal urge, can find its spontaneous encounter. Unlike our hands-off, manicured city parks, such a place should be crowded with every variety of trees, liberally strewn with moss-covered rocks, and filled with the "surprise" of little brooks and ponds.

Such wilderness areas would preserve small "pockets" of an America as she was in her unsettled and unexplored state. Better than any history book, children would learn from brooks and ponds to know and reverence water that, until some drought reminds us, is usually taken for granted. They would have a greater awareness of how trees become the timber and boards for the walls and furniture of our homes. The once ubiquitous berry would make a comeback. What can plant a better nostalgia than for children to stain their hands and mouths with wild strawberries, raspberries, blueberries to a symphony of bird song and humming insects? Millions of our children are culturally deprived even when they have had innumerable trips to museums and historic sites. How many have tasted a wild berry? I know that not *one* of my students has done so! These were the thoughts brought to me by my small resolve to search for a fresh, and more sane, perception through the quiet influence of a tree-cathedral.

Though I long for a wilder place, the tensions and trivialities of city existence seem hollow and purposeless and confining when compared to the free bird-calls I hear all around me. The great height of the pines where I am sitting, and the gnarled and ancient live oaks, speak to me of an even more ancient Architect. Until very recently, this was a wild spot. But the old trees were allowed to stand and became a small "Holy Land" behind the new church which was built close to the road, providing a natural

A WOMAN'S WALDEN

barrier between these woods and civilization. I have climbed that wild oak in the corner to see what the elevation and the interior of a tree would grant me. It was like a visit to the attic of a tree.

> *I leaned my head against its bark and heard the quiet hum of insects, and they reminded me of that "strong and beautiful bug which came out of the dry leaf of an old table of apple wood, which had stood in a farmer's kitchen for sixty years, first in Connecticut, and afterward in Massachusetts,—from an egg deposited in the living tree many years earlier still, as appeared by counting the annual layers beyond it; which was heard gnawing out for several weeks, hatched perchance by the heat of an urn. Who does not feel his faith in a resurrection and immortality strengthened by hearing this? Who knows what beautiful and winged life has been buried for ages under many concentric layers of woodenness in the dead dry life of society, deposited at first in the alburnum of the green and living tree, which has been gradually converted into the semblance of its well-seasoned tomb,—heard perchance gnawing out now for years by the astonished family of man, as they sat round the festive board,—may unexpectedly come forth from amidst society's most trivial and handselled furniture to enjoy its summer life at last.*[5]

In the attic of a tree my free hand took pleasure in intercepting a sunbeam. I was led to my own "higher latitudes," and found opening inside of me "new channels, not of trade, but of thought."

Upon returning to my house, I was brought down to earth, literally and figuratively, by a door-to-door salesman inviting me to buy a grave-plot. I refused on the grounds that I was too busy playing with the "coin" that energizes my own clay. To my children I say, "Do not look for me beneath some sculptured

"The Green Blade"

marker. I will return in pages where your eyes can pause at words that I have loved. I want the 'continents and seas' of my private world to invite you to explore places where I have been 'an isthmus or an inlet . . . the Atlantic and Pacific ocean of one's being alone,' "[6] places where I have had more of God than society could grant me.

"But you have to be practical," I was told by the economically minded. "Think what a zero year will do to your Social Security benefits. After all, you have not worked very long. Think of your teacher's pension; you have been teaching only twelve years. A decent pension requires at least twenty years!" The unbending facts of dollars and cents were a powerful argument against my taking a year off without salary. "What if you get sick?" was another argument made to dissuade me.

I remembered the "good old days" of the family doctor, before science decreed the era of the specialist. I mourn the passing of that one man who knew a little about many things pertaining to the total person. Now I am greeted by my medical man as an ear, a heart, a stomach, a uterus, a brain, a bladder, a limb. Indeed, in the emergency room of a hosptial attached to a city of no more than thirty thousand, I was once the recipient of the orderly's call to the supervisors and heard myself described, as he pushed me energetically in my wheel chair, "Here comes the knee!" Unfortunately, my knee could not be separated from the personality whose chemistry determines the health or sickness of its component parts.

As for rising medical costs, I remembered bringing my son with a broken leg to a general practitioner of twenty short years ago. X-rays, setting, diagnosis and cast came to a total of eighteen dollars. That leg still carries my six-foot-three-inch son. Five years ago, another simple break came to nearly two thousand dollars. A patient shunted from specialist to specialist found that within three months she had accumulated twenty thousand dollars in medical bills.

A WOMAN'S WALDEN

At her death bed she died believing her case had started with a professional oversight, a breakdown in communication between her "specialists." Such men are truly masters of their discipline, but in some corner of their solitude they too must suffer the scientific "amputation" of personality from its disorder.

Perhaps the most "modern" medical advice comes from Socrates, "who, advising his disciples to be solicitous of their health as a chief study, added that it was hard if a man of sense, having a care to his exercise and diet, did not better know than any physician what was good or ill for him" or, an equally "modern" authority: "Tiberius said that whoever had lived twenty years ought to be responsible to himself for all things that were wholesome or hurtful to him, and know how to order himself without physic."

Accordingly, I have become my own doctor, accepting the scornful rebuke from my own "specialist," who said, patronizingly, "And what medical school did you graduate from?" I do admit that I often wonder if my sunrise-to-sunset regimen, and my two-mile morning walk, plus housework, and outdoor gardening, accounts for my excellent health, or whether the confidence in my Adelle Davis self-medication is the real cause. Faith may be the truest placebo.

Being without health insurance, I am not fearful of institutional dying. Having no money assures me that I shall have my heart's desire in the case of terminal illness; namely, to die in my own bed. All I shall require from the medical profession in such an eventuality is a measure of relief from pain. I want no mechanical devices which would ensure an empty "prolongation of life." I am indeed, "a tool of tools" when I survive by means of tubes and electronic "helps." It cannot be even an approximation of life, except in terms of money; it keeps millions of medical personnel employed. My life's tangibles could become negotiable currency with which to pay for such a dubious longevity.

"The Green Blade"

However, overnight surgery has acquainted me with the animal-like pleading of persons in pain, and my two nights of listening to the clock-like regularity of a dying man's pleas (so the nurse informed me) sent me home physically improved, but forever pained in my heart. Definitely, I shall want assistance in bearing pain.

Interestingly, the fact that I cannot afford hospitalization insurance gives me a partial answer to the question, "Why should we cultivate poverty?" I see that by simply exploring my lack and need for insurance gives me another approach to dying. What new thoughts will other *needs* grant me?

Thoreau says, "Cultivate poverty like a garden herb, like sage,"[7] implying that a voluntary poverty, like the sage we once called wormwood, has a medicinal and corrective function, in which a little goes a long way. In contrast to what we ordinarily cultivate we are urged,

> *Do not trouble yourself much to get new things whether clothes or friends. Turn the old; return to them. Things do not change; we change. Sell your clothes and keep your thoughts. God will see that you do not lack society. If I were confined to a corner of a garret all my days, like a spider, the world would be just as large to me while I had my thoughts about me.*[8]

Have we, in our preoccupation with "getting and spending," sold our thoughts? Have we exchanged our thoughts for that perilous barter with "the cares of this life"? What will we gain by needing something and not getting it? By not getting that "new" thing, or friend we do, indeed, return to the old. We see them all with a heightened awareness. Ideas we did not know we were capable of thinking come to us unbidden.

I begin to understand that the old practice of penance was not an attempt to earn merit, but, rather, an identification with the

A WOMAN'S WALDEN

sufferings of One, who, through His poverty, made many rich. Like Him, we do not enrich others by sharing our wealth and our abundance. It is out of our needs, out of all the variations and forms that our poverty can take, that we enrich other lives. Wealth does no more than affirm our superiority over those with less. We obligate others to ourselves by what we dress up under the euphemism of generosity.

Need reduces us in the eyes of any who covet and admire wealth. In becoming poor we become anonymous, and lose at least some sense of our own importance. This ushers in an inverse sense of freedom. We are not cultivated socially, because we cannot or do not reciprocate in kind. We are cut off from a wide variety of influences that play upon our sensibilities and dissipate our energies. "The shadows of poverty and meanness gather around us, and lo! creation widens to our view."[9]

Shut up in the "isolation" of my deliberate experiment: not driving a car for one year (except for illness), having no phone, no T.V., going to no shopping center, attending no place of amusement, buying no new clothes, except shoes ($2.40 sneakers wore out before the year was out, and replacements cost $3.98). I have found that I lost nothing—no thing. Instead, my world has grown larger in my self-imposed exile. It is by the map of my own thoughts that I have traveled far.

> *Direct your thoughts inward, and you'll find*
> *A thousand regions in your mind*
> *Yet undiscovered. Travel them and be*
> *Expert in home-cosmography.*[10]

Yet thoughts can never be a substitute for life. My thoughts and my life are one. And, with regard to my "voluntary poverty," it must be understood that this is entirely different from the fear, anger, and frustration, and anxiety of men and women who see their children hungering. The Great Depression, and the terrible despair of genuine starvation, was a bitter and spirit-killing eclipse of many great minds that I have known from that generation. It was a time when the willingness to work brought many men little more than a W.P.A. pick and shovel. I cannot praise an *involuntary* poverty which "stifles the noblest thoughts in embryo."[11]

But what actually ushered in the "Golden Age" came to me at age six. A little immigrant girl's small-town wandering brought it about. In the tiny Minnesota town where we lived, my parents were occupied with making a living and mastering the mysteries of the English language. The social ostracism that foreign dresses and a strange name bring upon all children from the bird kingdom of the "ugly duckling," to Blacks, to Hispanics, to the present-day migrant worker, may or may not have contributed to my "accidental" discovery of the library story hour.

That open door remains open in memory, and from that discovery I entered the golden world. Mythology's sylvan landscape shaped my childish "crude" philosophy. From such irrational beginnings my emotions, my imagination, and my intellect were nourished. An uprooted child, brought to America at age three, I was to learn the truth of Schiller's words, "Deeper meaning resides in fairy tales told to me in childhood than in the truth that is taught by life."

From myths and fairy tales I learned:
> ... *that a struggle against severe difficulties in life is unavoidable, is an intrinsic part of human existence—but that if one does not shy away, but steadfastly meets unexpected and often unjust hardships one masters all obstacles and at the end emerges victorious.*
>
> *Modern stories written for young children mainly avoid these existential problems, although they are crucial issues for all of us. The child needs particularly to be given suggestions in symbolic form about how he*

A WOMAN'S WALDEN

may deal with these issues and grow safely into maturity. "Safe" stories mention neither death nor aging, the limits set to our existence, nor the wish for eternal life. The fairy tale, by contrast confronts the child squarely with the basic human predicament.[12]

What better way could I have learned about the infinite richness and diversity of life? What better way to learn that the *un*familiar need not be threatening? What better way to learn how to venture than through these early ventures, in the vicarious safety of a fairy tale?

It followed, then, that my life did not fall into a "beaten track" of tradition and conformity. The opening of my imagination at an early age provided me with a fantasy life that went beyond wish-fulfillment. I learned to experiment with possibilities both real and imaginary. A broad frame of reference gave me the freedom to build "castles in the air," which is where they belong. "Now put foundations under them."[13]

What are the foundations we place under "castles in the air"? Human experience will show us disappointments, pain, loneliness, weakness, failure, embarrassment, bereavement, and insecurity, yet the dream reminds us that it is our *interpretation* of all such experiences which enable us to live beyond them. We can turn them into the "coin" by which we will purchase the very future we envision. What we have tried and experienced becomes the medium of exchange on which we move to the *not yet tried*.

Because we see only the nearest link in the great chain of being, we think that our fate is static. But to believe that our fate is fixed is, as Epicurus has said, ". . . the worst kind of slavery." Rather, our fate is a continuous renewal. No, not a rah-rah-rah, simplistic, "all's-right-with-the-world" denial of troubling experiences, but renewal built upon contrast. "We are troubled . . . yet not distressed; . . . perplexed, but not in despair; persecuted, but not forsaken, cast down, but not destroyed."[14] Our outer self

"The Green Blade"

perishes daily while our inner self is renewed.

How can such a juxtaposition of experiences be termed renewal? Because "that Divinity which shapes our ends" takes the very poisons that would destroy us and turns them into vaccines for our healing. Does this operate for deliberate faults and failings? Yes, that thief who used his high position to seduce his employee's wife, and afterwards, sent him on a dangerous mission that would insure his death, is the best historical proof we need. One line in Psalm 51, King David's renewal prayer, says it for us: "Create in me a clean heart, O God; and renew a right spirit within me."[15] What finer "vaccine" can be cited? Why are the literal vaccines for small-pox and diptheria and polio easier to accept than the "absurdity" of a God who goes beyond mere pardon, and takes each failure, each mistake and makes them (the failures!) show forth His praise? Without such remaking renewal the best we could produce would be futile regret and a vague repentance in which we would never reform.

We accept the fact that our original personalities were beyond our powers to create. Even more impossible is it for us to recreate a broken resolve, or undo an injury, or call back an angry word. Faced with such impossibilities, we can mourn out of fear of consequences, knowing that God is no respector of person in the return of those injuries and words upon our own heads. We can mourn for a remembrance that will never leave us, and for our own impotence in forgetting, but such sorrow is neither repentance nor renewal. Similar recognition was also shared by Judas and led him to suicide. Other millions live out their life-long "suicides" in visible or invisible despair.

But the "other" repentance is re-creative. It is the wild logic of a God who builds our faith on such failures as King David, and that boastful, impulsive St. Peter. By slow stages we learn that repentance is not a single act, but a renewing process and a daily course to follow. Impossibilities induce us to say with David:

A WOMAN'S WALDEN

"Against thee, thee only have I sinned and done this evil in thy sight."[16] We must undeceive ourselves that there is any other way.

Spring teaches us the same lesson:
Nature is so rife with life that myriads can be sacrificed and suffered to prey on one another; that tender organizations can be so serenely squashed out of existence like pulp—tadpoles which herons gobble up, tortoises and toads run over in the road, and that sometimes it has rained flesh and blood! With the liability to accident, we must see how little account is to be made of it. The impression made on a wise man is that of universal innocence. Poison is not poison after all, nor are any wounds fatal. Compassion is a very tenable ground. It must be expeditious. Its pleadings will not bear to be stereotyped.[17]

Yet we stereotype both compassion and spring. Love is the only travel agent by which we can break the stereotype. We call this love by many names, and mistakenly endow it with the attributes of biochemistry, hate, jealousy, possessiveness, while it remains a love "perfumed with hope and power." Compounded from truth, it is not an abstraction that we can neither see nor touch. How could we know it apart from a direct experience? Someone says, "I'm telling you the truth," and you believe it because you see, and trust, the speaker. Similarly, I trust that Love which tells me, "I am the way, the truth and the life."[18] "I hearing get, who had but ears, And sight, who had but eyes before."[19] More, He opens my understanding.

I hope that "the volatile truth" of what I have here said, "betrays the inadequacy of the residual statement."[20]

When He speaks to me, He does not "level downward to our dullest perception always, and praise that as common sense."[21] A transformation that is not self-willed takes place, and I discover

"The Green Blade"

that His way and His truth have displaced common sense until my life is given *to* me; my common sense is not the deciding factor. Replaced by understanding, my common sense is able to let go. I can accept that I was made to be what I am. "A living dog is better than a dead lion," said Solomon. Thus I must attend a daily "funeral"; those experiences from which I had hoped to emerge as a heroic (not dead) lion require daily relinquishing. I learn what St. Paul meant when he said, "I die daily."[22] At the same time, I also receive Paul's answer, "My strength is made perfect in weakness."[23] Best of all, I move beyond the common sense need to decide what is best for my life. Since, in a real sense, He is the way, the truth and the life, my surrender to the truth of His claim can have no other words than "Not my life, but your life *in* me, not my will, but Thy will."

In this way alone I shall find: "Only that day dawns to which we are awake. There is more day to dawn. The sun is but a morning star."[24]

Poems

Why?

Reasons of the heart
Never by reason met,
Living by logic unreconciled
Mind's rival and mind's threat.

Reason never met by reason
Residing in the heart.
Known by an unknowing
Being's better part.

A WOMAN'S WALDEN

When Less Is More

Not till I see in more
The price demanded,
Can less be multiplied.
Not till a need not met
Makes of necessity invention
Can currency be cast way
For coin not of this realm.

And yet we tire of more and more
And more, as life is bartered
For a custom or a thing.
Reminding us of our denials,
Of our full hands,
Too full for prayer,
And those accumulations
For which we left our God
Where less is more.

Poems

Appearance and Reality
Luke 12:1b

Keep me from sacred jargon—
Parrot mouthed.
From speaking words,
I have been taught
But have not lived.

   Show me Thy truth,
   Must first possess
   The hidden, "inward part."
   Must deeply grow
   Into the dark and secret soil,
   Of my deceitful heart.

Possess—
What lies beneath,
All outward seeming.
And until then,
O keep me silent, Lord!

A WOMAN'S WALDEN

Spiritual Riddle

Not according to the deeds
   that I have done,
   but according to
   the mercy more abundant
   of my God.
This is the message
   that my life must show
   in gift conferred
   by His own power on those
   from sin's destruction saved.
In mundane view,
   prosaically involved
   with things called
   everyday,
   I have been born to show—
   not for some distant scene
   but now—
   just as I am
   and where,
   a wonder all improbable
   of weaknesses and sin,
   that in things so despised
   God never hides from view
   what He by grace can do!

Poems

The Broken Stone

Hast Thou not said
Thy stones in fairest colors
Shall be laid?
And am I not a pebble
Small and grey
Stone among stones
Upon a busy road?
Till one day, broken,
Thou did'st take me up
To smite the broken parts,
And lo, both fire and heat
Came forth in fair-hued flames,
In warmth none could have known
Was there.

A WOMAN'S WALDEN

Insight

Frost-fallen are the leaves
  that turn bare branches
  into traceries of lace
    against the sky,
  and not till then
     did I
  the shape of trees
  more fully know.
Dismantled of green contours
  all the gnarled and bent
    groan greyly
  for their final cloak
  of fringe-flaked snow.

How like the heart
    by life's short spring and summer
     greenly gowned,
all scarcely known
  till scarlet autumn ends
  with winter's leaflessness,
    and then we stand
  stripped strangely in sad shapes
     life-long our own;
  in such unrealized reality
    the eyes that saw
    but saw not say,
    "I never knew this was the way
     her heart would look."

Poems

Orbed Peril

Light leaps toward light
Where sunlight falls
On white and shoreless sand,
But where dark images rise up
To break the beams of light
With tree-branch supplications
Or jagged, glacial rock,
There
Sunlight falls in fragments
Sifting softly through dark leaves
Or brightening ravines
Of sharply shaded spires,
Telling my heart
Its life-light falls
Through darker images
In broken rays
More merciful than light
Whose full-orbed fall
Would turn the heart
To barren, burning sand.

A WOMAN'S WALDEN

From Bone to Flint

This stony dust
   from which my bones were made
     will petrify to flint
       like ancient logs
        that have become
  a wonderment of rosy stone
    from their long death
 in water-buried bogs,
where every circled year
    of their recorded growth
 is an event held fast
    in those remembering rocks.

And still not every tree
    is so preserved,
   not every tree or human frame
     to flint returns.
Some trees decay, some burn,
  some die and dwindle.
But my last journey
    will from bone to flint be made
because I died and fell
   where tears had fallen
long before I came to be.

In that wild alchemy
    of nature's scheme, these
   turn the burning bones to flint
    in water-buried places
     and there—
there creates their resurrection
    into flint-born flame.

Touched in the Hollow of the Thigh

To limp forever, Lord?
Forever bear the sign of conflict lost?
In this Thy will for me?
As one with night-concealed assailant
Wrestled in the dark
So have I held to Thee
When all was night
Yet gladly will I halting walk
And marks of chastening bear,
If
In the place of my defeats,
Thou wilt with Jacob
Bless me there.

A WOMAN'S WALDEN

Missile

Not without shuddering
Will wings wind-lifted
Fly.
The riveted, quivering silver
Screams its still-voiced struggle
To be air-borne.
Climbing the vapor ladders
Of the sky,
This metal bird flies only
As its motored convolutions
Strain at currents
Of white scattered mists,
All unsubstantial
To frail, fingered hands.
Yet power groans at gravity
To gain those higher heights
Not given hands to know.

Poems

Love's Response

Small sounds will waken me—
The groping sounds
Of small hands on a sheet,
The murmur
Of a baby's quick drawn breath
Through tiny lips
That shape earth's sweetest word.
By this I know in part
How God
In tenderest love responds
When feebly our first call
Is shaped for Him!

A WOMAN'S WALDEN

Strange Gifts of the Magi

Taught by stars—
How did they know,
How did they understand
Enough to bring
Gifts of gold and frankincense
And myrrh?

Taught by Thyself—
Teach us to bring
Unto Thy least
As unto Thee
Gifts like theirs—
The costliest.

Teach us to bring
Love's gold
Not
For advantage or exchange.
And friendship's
Frankincense
Fragrant through use alone.
Show us
The meaning of myrrh
By ancients used for wounds,
And teach us as we walk
Through this world's wounds,
To give, as Thou dids't give,
Ourselves.

Poems

Twentieth Century Christmas Carol

They will say that my heart had no song
Save the harsh sounds of metal on metal
That my fingers could frame no new words
Between their unceasing tattoo
On the round keys of dollars and cents,
But that was the "tune" demanded
For translated gifts of gold,
And my love in its perishing laces and plush
Became incense and myrrh
On doll's faces and such.

A WOMAN'S WALDEN

Monterey Cypress

Wild, wild contorted tree,
Bent by an unequal strength
Of winds that lash at broken, sea-girt rocks.
Howling discontent
That changes shape of shore and stone,
That grapples with young, supple trees
Skyward inclined; till bending low
They bow, and bowing bind themselves with beauty
With wind snared in their branches
And there forever stilled.

Poems

Home For Dinner

He said,
I guess I am not hungry
While every word fell flat,
And she, with tightened lips,
Built walls around her words.
They sat in awkward silence,
Each searching for new ways
To fill a cumbrous pause,
Until one chair
Pushed quietly away,
Made speech by being empty.

A WOMAN'S WALDEN

Cold Comfort

The ridicule remains
And scorn its hiss retains.
Show me in letters high
Late praises lie,
And like a mocking echo sung
Re-echoes with no tongue.

Poems

The Evolution of Letters

A penny stamp once held my heart
Those words by which I lived:
Nonsense or surprise,
Disappointment or sorrow,
Ruin or unanticipated good.
O Love, I wait for mail
Though penny stamps are past.
Gone
Like words that never come.

A WOMAN'S WALDEN

Heather

They set the grey rocks flaming
To burn the purple heather
That blooms, where the wildest of oceans
Sets boulders gnashing at boulders;
For in niches of wounded granite
The lowly heather flames.

From wounds that I did not inflict
A brittle bloom is flaming
To leave ashes for another's flame,
Yet over my grave I shall sing
Of the dust-borne heather that grows
In the creviced stone-set mountains.

Poems

Reading the Green

There are hills beyond the hills,
Beyond the hills that I have climbed,
And that first hill's stony crest
Gave me visions of the next.
I had thought the hills were measured
From day's dawn to day's downfall,
For the strength of every climber
From decrees to climbers all.

Slow ascent first hills command,
Not by heights but unmet slopes,
And the morning sun moves slowly
When compared with morning hopes.
Hills that follow from that first one
Find their summits quickly climbed,
If the view from that first hilltop
Is with strength and morning timed.

But the hills that follow hills
Stretch to life's late afternoon;
One more summit, one more summit,
Is the climber's cairn or rune.
Yet the hills that face the sundown
Must be climbed as light grows dark
And we pass the granite markers
With a painful, aching heart.

Not till then we note the stillness
As our hills to mountains grow.
Not till then we note the crevice
We must cross to peaks of snow.

A WOMAN'S WALDEN

Grace Notes

A murmur that is melody
From invisible fingers touched,
Sounds in the pointed pines
Like breath strokes against strings.
But in the weeping birches
Liquid rhythms whisper
As leaf and limbs alike
Languorous and lingering
Add their grace notes
To the music of the spheres.

Poems

The Lawn Mower

I see the weighted wheels
And the inexorable blades
That nothing green and growing can resist.
And yet I walk on dandelions
Whose strength is to persist.

A WOMAN'S WALDEN

The Beating

Not larks alone—
All things were made for flight:
The feathered wave
The wing-tipped pine
The wind-borne flame;
For the wings of what we would be
Are beating, beating, beating
Beneath the wings of what we are.

Poems

The White Heron

Was it our tranquil calm
That brought you motionless before us?
Majestic in your statued grace,
With elegance of stance
In polished whiteness
Like opalescent moon-glow
Against the tangled green
Of mangrove's land-building roots?

Here, coral fragments
And skeletons of seas
Bring forth an earth new-made.
Like old invaders of the deep,
The mangrove strides across sea-shallows
Drawing to its own
A still lagoon of dreamlike peace
And this snowy, lone white heron.

Notes

Chapter 1
"Delicate Handling"
1. *Walden*, p. 9.
2. Isaiah 30:7 (KJV).
3. *Walden*, p. 61.
4. *Walden*, p. 30.
5. *Ibid.*, p. 9.
6. *Op. Cit.*, p. 8, 9.
7. Proverbs 23:7 (KJV).

Chapter 2
"Thumbnail Living"
1. *Walden*, p. 66.
2. *Ibid.*, p. 25.
3. Job 5:7 (KJV).
4. Charlotte Brontë, *The Self Conceived*, Helen Morgan (W.W. Norton, New York), p. 256.
5. *Walden*, p. 22.

Chapter 3
At a Standstill
1. *Walden*, p. 79.
2. *Ibid.*, p. 12.
3. Gerard Manley Hopkins, *The Poems of Gerard Manley Hopkins*, edited by W.H. Gardner and N.H. Mackenzie (Oxford University Press, 1967), p. 66.
4. *Ibid.*, p. 66.
5. *Op. Cit.*, p. 66.

Chapter 4
Home: Our First Paradise
1. *Walden*, p. 23.
2. *Walden*, p. 24.

A WOMAN'S WALDEN

Chapter 5
"Where I Lived and What I Lived For"
1. *Walden*, p. 66.
2. Jeremiah 4:22 (KJV).
3. *Walden*, p. 60.
4. *Ibid.*, p. 61.
5. John 3:8 (KJV).
6. Lamentations 3:23 (KJV).
7. *Walden*, p. 65.
8. *Ibid.*, p. 65.
9. *Op. Cit.*, p. 67.
10. *Op. Cit.*, p. 66.
11. *Great Books Syntopicon*, p. 886.
12. *Walden*, p. 70.
13. Philippians 4:7 (KJV).
14. Psalm 46:10 (KJV).
15. Genesis 4:1 (KJV).

Chapter 6
Reading
1. *Walden*, p. 76.
2. *Ibid.*, p. 72.
3. *Op. Cit.*, p. 73.
4. Isaiah 43:2; 42:16 (AMP).
5. *Walden*, p. 76.

Chapter 7
Leisure
1. *Walden*, p. 65.
2. Psalm 65:8 (KJV).
3. *The Poems of Gerard Manley Hopkins*, "The Golden Echo," (Oxford University Press, New York, London, Toronto, 1967), pp. 92-93.
4. *Walden*, p. 79.
5. *The Selected Writings of R.W. Emerson*, ed. Brooks Atkinson, (Random House Publishers, New York: 1950), pp. 11-13.
6. Proverbs 23:7 (KJV).
7. *Walden*, p. 84.
8. Psalm 127:2 (KJV).
9. Isaiah 53:12 (KJV).

Chapter 8
Socializing
1. *Walden*, p. 98.
2. *Ibid.*, p. 98.

Notes

Chapter 8
(continued)

3 *Op. Cit.*, p. 98.
4 Alvin Toffler, *Future Shock* (Random House, New York, 1970), p. 117.

Chapter 9
Guests
1 *Walden*, p. 93.
2 Alvin Toffler, *Future Shock* (Random House, New York, 1970), p. 117.
3 Isaiah 58:4, 6-8 (KJV).
4 *Walden*, p. 102.
5 *Ibid.*, p. 102.
6 Louis Untermeyer, *Modern British Poetry* (Harcourt, Brace and World, New York, 1962), p. 615.
7 Luke 24:35 (KJV).

Chapter 10
Gardening
1 *Walden*, p. 97.
2 *Ibid.*, p. 107.
3 *The Selected Writings of R.W. Emerson*, ed. Brooks Atkinson, (Random House Publishers, New York: 1950), p. 12.
4 *Walden*, p. 108.
5 *Emerson*, p. 13.
6 *Walden*, p. 114.
7 *Ibid.*, p. 114.
8 *The Golden Bough*, Sir James George Frazer, (Macmillan Co., New York: 1971), pp. 820-21.
9 *Walden*, pp. 111-112.
10 *Ibid.*, p. 113.
11 *Emerson*, p. 23.

Chapter 11
Neighbors
1 *Walden*, p. 216.
2 *Basic Gardening Illustrated* (Lane Books, Menlo Park, California, 1971).

Chapter 12
Retirement Village, U.S.A.
1 *Walden*, p. 214.
2 Exodus 20:12 (KJV).

A WOMAN'S WALDEN

Chapter 13
Former Inhabitants
1. *Walden*, p. 248.
2. *West Pasco's Heritage* (West Pasco Historical Society, 1974), p. 280.
3. *Ibid.*, p. 299.
4. *The Florida of the Inca*, Inca, Garcilosa de la Vega, Translated and edited by John Grier and Jeannette Johnson Varner (University of Texas Press, Austin, 1951), pp. 19-22.
5. *Ibid.*, p. 360.
6. *Op. Cit.*, pp. 373-377.
7. *Op. Cit.*, p. 620.
8. *Op. Cit.*, p. 619.
9. *Op. Cit.*, p. 631.
10. *Op. Cit.*, p. 631.

Chapter 14
The Pond
1. *Walden*, p. 189.
2. *Ibid.*, p. 129.
3. Isaiah 28:10 (KJV).

Chapter 15
Jack's Pond
1. *Walden*, p. 106.

Chapter 16
Dual Urges
1. *Walden*, pp. 148-150.
2. *Ibid.*, p. 143.
3. Psalm 55:6 (KJV).
4. Romans 7:18, 19 (KJV).
5. *Walden*, p. 148.
6. Romans 7:14 (KJV).
7. *Walden*, pp. 148-150.
8. Matthew 15:11 (KJV).
9. *Walden* p. 146.
10. *Ibid.*, p. 143.
11. *Ibid.*, p. 150.
12. Matthew 17:21 (KJV).
13. *Walden*, p. 146.
14. Luke 18:11 (KJV).
15. Romans 7:18 (KJV).
16. 1 Corinthians 9:27 (KJV).
17. *Walden*, p. 151.

Notes

Chapter 17
The "Smoke-Self"
1. *Walden*, p. 213.
2. *Ibid.*, p. 118.
3. Shakespeare, *Hamlet*, III, i.
4. Mark 5:19 (KJV).
5. 1 Corinthians 2:12b (KJV).
6. Isaiah 42:16 (KJV).
7. Proverbs 23:7 (KJV).
8. Thomas Merton, *Thoughts in Solitude* (Dell Publishing Co., New York, 1961), p. 45.
9. *Ibid.*, p. 31.

Chapter 18
Symbolic Activities
1. *Walden*, p. 246.
2. James 1:17 (KJV).
3. Hymn, "Abide With Me."
4. *Walden*, p. 163.
5. *Seeds of Contemplation*, by Thomas Merton (New Directions Press, 1949), p. 136.
6. John 15:12 (KJV).
7. Matthew 10:37 (KJV).
8. Luke 24:35 (KJV).
9. 1 Timothy 5:8 (KJV).
10. Matthew 6:6 (KJV).
11. Psalm 46:10 (KJV).
12. *Walden*, p. 164.
13. Matthew 7:2 (KJV).
14. Matthew 25:35, 40 (KJV).

Chapter 19
Summer Locked Up
1. *Walden*, pp. 194, 195.
2. *Ibid.*, p. 194.
3. *Op. Cit.*, p. 194.
4. Psalm 19:3 (KJV).
5. William Wordsworth, *Trio: A Book of Stories, Plays, Poems*, edited by Harold P. Simonson (Harper and Row, Publishers, New York, 1980), p. 614.
6. *Walden*, p. 198.
7. *Ibid.*, p. 198.
8. Revelation 21:5 (KJV).
9. *The Selected Writings of R.W. Emerson*, edited by Brooks Atkinson (Random House Publishers, 1950), p. 191.

A WOMAN'S WALDEN

Chapter 20
"The Green Blade"
1. *Walden*, pp. 241-242.
2. *Ibid.*, pp. 203-204.
3. *Op. Cit.*, p. 121.
4. Ephesians 3:20 (KJV).
5. *Walden*, p. 221.
6. *Ibid.*, p. 213.
7. *Op. Cit.*, p. 218.
8. *Op. Cit.*, p. 218.
9. *Op. Cit.*, p. 218.
10. *Op. Cit.*, p. 213.
11. *The Uses of Enchantment*, Bruno Bettelheim (Alfred A. Knopf, Inc., New York: 1977), p. 5.
12. *Ibid.*, p. 8.
13. *Walden*, p. 215.
14. 2 Corinthians 4:8 (KJV).
15. Psalm 51:10 (KJV).
16. Psalm 51:4 (KJV).
17. *Walden*, p. 211.
18. John 14:6 (KJV).
19. *Walden*, p. 246.
20. *Ibid.*, p. 215.
21. *Op. Cit.*, pp. 215, 216.
22. 1 Corinthians 15:31 (KJV).
23. 2 Corinthians 12:9 (KJV).
24. *Walden*, p. 221.